Learning About Bibl

Bible People

of Faith

For Intergenerational Use

by
Marcia Joslin Stoner

Abingdon Press

Nashville

Bible People of Faith
Learning About Bible People
For Intergenerational Use

Requests for permission should be submitted in writing to:
Rights and Permissions, The United Methodist Publishing House,
201 Eighth Avenue South, P.O. Box 801, Nashville, TN 37203; faxed to (615) 749-6128;
or submitted via e-mail to permissions@abingdonpress.com.

Credits are listed on page 157.

ISBN 9780687642380

07 08 09 10 11 12 13 14 15 16 — 10 9 8 7 6 5 4 3 2 1

MANUFACTURED IN THE UNITED STATES OF AMERICA

Table of Contents

How to Use This Book-

This book is a reference book, an art book, and an activity book. It is meant primarily for ten-year-olds through adult, though there are a few activities that can be adapted for younger age levels.

FOR PRETEEN AND YOUTH ACTIVITIES

Information About Bible People—Share some of the background of the people of the Bible as they are studied on a regular basis. If you are doing a Bible survey, use the portraits in the front and back of the book to make a pictorial timeline.

Additional Activities—You may wish to supplement current studies with one or more of the activities in this book.

Stewardship Retreat—The "Day Retreat—Let's Form a Faith Community" on pages 120 & 122 makes a good study for tweens and youth to complement your church's stewardship drive. If you wish to make it into a weekend retreat, pair this activity with some of the stewardship activities from *Tween Spirituality: Offering Opportunities in Preteen Spiritual Growth,* © 2003 Abingdon Press, ISBN 9780687075515.

FOR INTERGENERATIONAL ACTIVITIES

Third Grade Through Adult—Many activities in this book require an ability to read, so those in the third grade and up are best suited to appreciate the activities in the entire book. Let more-sophisticated readers work with less-sophisticated readers. *Some activities require abstract thinking skills and are most appropriate for the preteen level and beyond.*

Kindergarten Through Adult—"The Bible People Art Gallery," some of the Christmas activities, and some service projects are the only ones that are really appropriate for children below third grade.

FOR SHORT-TERM INTERGENERATIONAL EVENTS

Use the reproducible "Lesson Plan Form" on page 6 to set up Advent sessions for all age levels. Try to form intergenerational groups that contain members of every age level.

The "Day Retreat—Let's Form a Faith Community" on pages 120 & 122 is perfect for intergenerational use, especially fifth grade through adult. Again, if you pair it with **Tween Spirituality** *(see "Stewardship Retreat" above), you can easily have a weekend retreat for preteens through adults.*

Bible People of Fait

Sample Lesson Plan

*This sample lesson plan is based on one possible way
a class could use this book for a lesson.*

SESSION TIME: 1 hour

ARRIVAL ACTIVITY: Two or three early arrivals make frame for Solomon's portrait, pp. 28, 30, & 32. Let another make a title for the picture to hang under it.
Supplies to gather: colored construction paper, glue, scissors, ruler, glitter
pplies to get / things to do: Buy white art paper. Cut out Solomon's portrait, p. 15.

OPENING ACTIVITY: Read today's Bible story: 1 Kings 3:16-28.
Supplies to gather: Bibles
pplies to get / things to do:

MAIN ACTIVITY: Have a short discussion of the wisdom of Solomon's choice. Then discuss how we make choices.
Supplies to gather: Bibles
pplies to get / things to do:

GAME: "Wise Choices Game," p. 52 (bottom)
Supplies to gather: 8½-by-11 sheets of paper (4 for each participant)
pplies to get / things to do: Make copies of "Wise Choice Game Cards," p. 54 and top of p. 55.

CRAFT: None today
Supplies to gather:
pplies to get / things to do:

MISSIONS: None today. Substitute clip from *Ice Age.*
Supplies to gather: DVD and TV
pplies to get / things to do: Call Judy J. at the church office to make sure we have licensing agreement.

MUSIC: Combine with worship
Supplies to gather: Tom B. (Make sure piano is in place for him.)
pplies to get / things to do: Ask youth to carry hymnals from sanctuary to classroom.

WORSHIP: Use *Upper Room Devotional* for the day. Add music and prayer.
Supplies to gather: *Upper Room Devotional*
pplies to get / things to do: See "Music" above.

What have I forgotten?

Lesson Plan Form

SESSION TIME _____

ARRIVAL ACTIVITY: _____
Supplies to gather: _____
Supplies to get / things to do: _____
_____

OPENING ACTIVITY: _____
Supplies to gather: _____
Supplies to get / things to do: _____
_____

MAIN ACTIVITY: _____
Supplies to gather: _____
Supplies to get / things to do: _____
_____

GAME: _____
Supplies to gather: _____
Supplies to get / things to do: _____
_____

CRAFT: _____
Supplies to gather: _____
Supplies to get / things to do: _____
_____

MISSIONS: _____
Supplies to gather: _____
Supplies to get / things to do: _____
_____

MUSIC: _____
Supplies to gather: _____
Supplies to get / things to do: _____
_____

WORSHIP: _____
Supplies to gather: _____
Supplies to get / things to do: _____
_____

What have I forgotten? _____
_____
_____

ABRAHAM AND SARAH

REBEKAH

ISAAC

Bible People of Faith

ESAU   JACOB

JOSHUA   RACHEL

Bible People of Faith

JOSEPH

MOSES

Bible People of Faith

GIDEON

DEBORAH

SAMUEL

SAMSON

SOLOMON

SAUL

DAVID

Bible People of Faith

ESTHER

RUTH

EZRA

JOB

JONAH   DANIEL

NEHEMIAH   JEREMIAH

Bible People of Faith

ISAIAH   HULDAH

ELIJAH

Old Testament
Patriarchs
and
Matriarchs

ADAM AND EVE
Adam *means* **earth** *or* **earthy;** Eve *means* **the mother of all living**. *Some later traditions say that* **Eve** *comes from the word* **serpent**.

There are two biblical accounts of the creation of man and woman. In Genesis 1:27-30 God created male and female. God blessed them and gave them dominion over the air, sea, and earth. In Genesis 2:4-25 Adam was created, and God created the animals in order to give Adam a partner. God decided this wasn't good enough, so God created woman from Adam's rib. Since these accounts were written long before history was recorded as we know it, exact details were not as important to believers as they are today. What was important was that God was the creator.

Adam and Eve were together when Eve was addressed by the serpent, so Adam heard the exchange (Genesis 3:6). Even if he hadn't been with her, Adam could have refused to participate. Later traditions ignore that and place all the blame on Eve.

CAIN, ABEL, AND SETH
The three sons of Adam and Eve. Cain was a tiller of the ground, and Abel was a keeper of sheep (Genesis 4:1-2). When they offered a sacrifice to God, Abel's was accepted but Cain's was not. Though the reason for rejection is not stated, verse 7 implies that God knew there was sin in Cain's heart.

Cain did not react well to God's rebuke. He lured Abel out to a field and killed him. Worse than that, he tried denying it and shifting responsibility to God, saying, "Am I my brother's keeper?" (verse 9). Cain was condemned to be a wanderer. However, God marked his forehead to protect him from others who might seek vengeance.

Seth was born as God's replacement for Abel. Seth, who died at the age of 912 (Genesis 5:8), is the ancestor of Noah.

NOAH
The story of Noah is a lengthy one that begins with the wickedness of humankind in Genesis 6 and goes through the descendants of Noah in Genesis 10.

Noah was basically humankind's second chance. He is sometimes considered the new Adam, a lone, righteous man called by God to build an ark, rescuing the animals of the earth and his own family from a devastating flood. God made a covenant with Noah. The sign of this covenant is the rainbow, the promise never again to cut off the whole earth with a great flood (Genesis 9:8-17). God blessed Noah and his sons and told them to "Be fruitful and multiply, and fill the earth" (Genesis 9:1). Noah lived to be 950 years old (Genesis 9:28-29).

Noah's sons were Shem, Ham, and Japheth. Abraham was descended from the line of Shem. (See pages 25 and 84.)

Bible People of Faith

ABRAHAM *The first patriarch. His father was Terah, descended from Noah. His name was originally* **Abram** *(meaning* **the father is exalted***). Born in Ur. Called by God to be the father of a people. No reason is given for the selection of Abram, but there is a tradition that his father was an idol maker and that Abram rejected the power of the idols. Abram's name was changed to* **Abraham** *(meaning* **father of a multitude***).*

Abraham is the founding patriarch of three of the world's great religions. Jews trace their ancestry through Isaac, the long-awaited son of Abraham and Sarah. Muslims trace their ancestry through Ishmael, the son of Abraham and Hagar. Christians claim Abraham as a patriarch through faith (Galatians 3:6-7, 29).

SARAH *Wife of Abraham. They were married in Ur. Originally named* **Sarai** *(meaning* **my princess***), her name was also changed at the time of the covenant to* **Sarah** *(meaning* **princess***, a more universal meaning). When Sarah remained childless, she pushed Abraham into having a child by Hagar. Then when Isaac was born, she became jealous of the attention Ishmael (Hagar's son) got and had Abraham send Hagar and Ishmael away.*

Sarah died at the age of 127 (Genesis 23:1).

Outline of Abraham and Sarah's Story

- Abram is born in Ur (Genesis 11:27-32).

- Abram (age 75) is called by God to depart Haran and go to the land God would show him. With him go his wife, Sarai, and his nephew Lot. They go to Canaan. God declares this the land he will give to Abram. Abram builds an altar (Genesis 12:1-9).

- Due to famine Abram and Sarai go to Egypt (Genesis 12:10-20).

- Abram, Sarai, and Lot leave Egypt and go into the Negeb. They are rich and must divide the land. Lot chooses the rich plain of the Jordan, near Sodom. Abram settles by the oaks of Mamre at Hebron. He builds an altar to the Lord there (Genesis 13).

- Sodom is invaded and Abram rescues Lot (Genesis 14).

- Abram is blessed by Melchizedek, king of Salem, but refuses to take gifts from the king (Genesis 14:17-24).

- Because of Abram's faithfulness, God promises him great numbers of descendants (Genesis 15).

- Birth of Abram's first son, Ishmael, by Hagar, a slave-girl. Abram is 86 years old (Genesis 16).

- The Lord makes a covenant with Abram (age 99) that he will be the father of a multitude of nations. The sign of the covenant is circumcision. Abram and Sarai are renamed Abraham and Sarah (age 90) and are promised a son they are to name Isaac (Genesis 17:1–18:15).

- Because Abraham pleads with God to save the city of Sodom if righteous people can be found, Lot is saved from the city (Genesis 18:16–19:29).

- Isaac is born. Abraham is 100 and Sarah going on 91 years old (Genesis 17:17; 21:1-7).

- Hagar and Ishmael are exiled (Genesis 21:8-20).

- Abraham makes peace with Abimelech (Genesis 21:22-34).

- Abraham is asked to sacrifice Isaac. As Abraham prepares to sacrifice Isaac, God sends a ram to take Isaac's place (Genesis 22).

- Sarah dies at 127. She is buried in a field east of Mamre purchased by Abraham (Genesis 23).

- Abraham dies at 175 and is buried next to Sarah by his sons Isaac and Ishmael (Genesis 25:7-10).

Activity: Bible People Portrait Gallery

Use the portraits found on pages 7-21 and pages 141-153 to make a dramatic Bible People Portrait Gallery for your classroom, hallway, or fellowship hall. If you are having a big event, assign a biblical person to one or two participants to design and prepare a frame. If you are doing an ongoing study, add to the gallery each week.

Cut apart the portraits and frame each separately, except for page 141 (the twelve disciples). That page is meant to be framed as if it were a class photograph like the ones seen on the walls of many high schools. The name of each person is on the back of the portraits so that you will know who they are when cut apart. Be sure to label the pictures in your portrait gallery.

For display space you may wish to use blank walls, folding screens, or even painted cardboard panels made from appliance boxes that can be free-standing in the room.

The art in this book has been done by a collection of artists, much as you would find in a museum. You may make all the frames look exactly alike, or you may wish to decorate each differently. If you use different frames for each portrait, there are suggestions on pages 30 and 32 for making unusual frames.

POSSIBLE USES OF GALLERY:

1. Pictorial timeline of the Bible

2. As a way to review Bible people as you learn about them

3. Decoration for a bare classroom or hallway

4. Fun craft activity

5. As an arrival activity for those waiting for others to come before beginning sessions

6. Any combination of the above

ISAAC (*meaning* **he laughs**) *Isaac, the second patriarch, is best known for three things: his near sacrifice by his father; his marriage to Rebekah producing twin sons, Jacob and Esau; and, because he was old and blind, being tricked into giving Jacob, the younger son, the blessing meant for Esau, the elder son. Isaac was a nomad like his father, Abraham, but he never left Canaan.*

REBEKAH *Wife of Isaac. Mother of Jacob and Esau. Sister of Laban. Daughter of Bethuel, who was the son of Abraham's younger brother Nahor. This makes Isaac and Rebekah cousins. She was sought out by Abraham's servant to be Isaac's wife. She married Isaac, and for twenty years she was childless (Genesis 25:19-26).*

When Rebekah finally became pregnant, she had a difficult time with her pregnancy. God told her that she was carrying two nations, and they were already struggling. Rebekah encouraged and tutored Jacob, her favorite, in how to trick Isaac into giving him Esau's blessing. Because of Esau's anger, she sent Jacob to her brother Laban. She never saw her beloved son again. Rebekah is often thought of as a schemer, but we must keep in mind that she was aware of God's intention for her younger son (Genesis 25:23), and this probably greatly affected her actions.

Outline of Isaac and Rebekah's Story

- Isaac is born (Genesis 21:1-7).

- Abraham is commanded to sacrifice Isaac. When Abraham prepares to obey, God sends a ram for the sacrifice (Genesis 22:1-19).

- Isaac (aged 40) marries Rebekah (Genesis 24).

- Isaac joins his half-brother Ishmael in burying Abraham, their father (Genesis 25:7-10).

- Twenty years after their marriage Rebekah gives birth to twins, Esau and Jacob (Genesis 25:19-26). Esau is Isaac's favorite son, but Jacob is Rebekah's favorite (Genesis 25:27-28).

- There is a famine in the land, but at God's command Isaac goes to Gerar, not Egypt. King Abimelech is impressed with how the Lord is with Isaac, and they agree to live peacefully (Genesis 26:1-33).

- Isaac is old and cannot see well (maybe advanced cataracts). He is tricked by his wife, Rebekah, and his son Jacob into giving Jacob the blessing meant for Esau (Genesis 27:1-29).

- Isaac gives Esau a new blessing (Genesis 27:30-40).

- Rebekah urges Jacob to flee Esau's fury (Genesis 27:41-46).

- Isaac dies at the age of 180. Esau and Jacob bury him (Genesis 35:27-28).

- Rebekah's death is not recorded in the Bible, but she is buried with Isaac, Abraham, and Sarah in the family burial site (Genesis 49:31).

Activity: Making Basic Frames

Frames for your Bible People Portrait Gallery can be as simple or as elaborate as you choose to make them.

1. For easy-to-make "frames," you may simply wish to decorate pieces of posterboard and glue the portraits in the middle of the finished posterboard.

2. Simple frames may be made by gluing each portrait to a piece of posterboard or construction paper a little larger than the portrait, giving a "border" to each portrait. A frame may then be constructed out of strips of construction paper and glued to the border of the portrait.

3. Begin framing each portrait by gluing the portrait to either posterboard or art paper, making sure that there are from two to three inches of posterboard or paper on each side of the portrait. You can then begin matting each portrait with different colored paper (construction or art paper), as many mats as you desire (probably one to three). Then make the outer frame from heavier paper or a different color of posterboard. Be sure to miter the corners (cut edges at angles and butt them up against each other).

4. Another option is to make the frame for each portrait by using small wooden frames, but this is expensive and can add considerably to the weight of the portrait.

Whatever framing method you choose, be sure to consider where and how you will be hanging the portraits. You don't want to use a method that will cause the picture to be heavier than you will have the ability to hang.

NOTE: The new temporary pull-tab hangers for pictures work very well on many different types of walls, even those made of concrete blocks.

Pages 30 and 32 offer some suggestions for decorating frames or mats.

JACOB *(meaning **grabber, heel, grabber of the heel, may God protect**, or variations of these depending upon the source)*

Jacob was a pivotal patriarch in the development of the Jewish people.

*Jacob had much to commend him. He had an ongoing relationship with God, even struggling with God in the form of a man. Because of this he was renamed **Israel**, meaning he had "striven with God and with humans, and [had] prevailed" (Genesis 32:28). Jacob was hard working and sometimes very patient, laboring for seven years to marry Rachel. When tricked by his uncle into marrying her sister Leah instead, he worked another seven years to marry Rachel. Jacob was also the father of the ancestors of the twelve tribes of Israel. Jacob was the carrier of God's promise to Abraham, Isaac, and the next generation.*

But don't put Jacob on too high of a pedestal! Jacob had many character flaws, and they resulted in harm to others. Jacob tricked his brother into signing over his birthright by playing on an obvious weakness of Esau's. Then, with the encouragement and help of his mother, he tricked his twin brother, defrauding him of his inheritance. Jacob did not have to act this way; God had already chosen him as the carrier of the promise to the next generation (Genesis 25:23) before he was born. Jacob pulled a slick stunt with Laban, his uncle, in order to build up his own herd. (Laban was a trickster himself.) And Jacob played favorites with his own sons. Though he had twelve sons (and one daughter, Dinah), he favored Rachel's sons, Joseph and Benjamin, over the others. His gift of a robe with long sleeves to Joseph (Genesis 37:3) helped further inflame his other sons and led to Joseph's being sold to Ishmaelite traders (Genesis 37:25-28).

Outline of Jacob's Story

• Esau and Jacob struggle in their mother's womb (Genesis 25:19-23).	• Jacob tricks Laban into giving him the best of his flocks. Jacob flees with his family. Laban catches up to him and they make a pact (Genesis 30:25–31:55).
• Esau and Jacob are born (Genesis 25:24-26).	• Jacob sends presents ahead to appease Esau (Genesis 32:3-21).
• Jacob buys Esau's birthright (Genesis 25:29-34).	
• Isaac is deceived by Jacob and Rebekah into giving Esau's blessing to Jacob (Genesis 27:1-29).	• Jacob wrestles with God in the form of a man at Peniel. He is blessed by God and given the name *Israel* (Genesis 32:22-32).
• Jacob escapes from an angry Esau and is sent to his uncle Laban's home (Genesis 27:41–28:5).	• Jacob and Esau reconcile (Genesis 33).
• Jacob dreams of a ladder with the top reaching heaven. Jacob is told by God that he and his offspring will be given the land before him (Genesis 28:10-22).	• Jacob gives his son Joseph a robe with long sleeves (Genesis 37:3). Jacob grieves when presented with the bloody robe (Genesis 37:29-36).
	• Jacob moves his family to Egypt (Genesis 46).
• Jacob works seven years to marry Rachel, but is tricked by Laban into marrying Leah instead. Then he works seven more years and marries Rachel. There is jealousy between his wives; Leah is unloved and Rachel is childless (Genesis 29–30).	• Jacob blesses Joseph's sons (Genesis 48).
	• Jacob dies and is buried beside Abraham, Sarah, Isaac, Rebekah, and Leah (Genesis 49:29–50:13).

Activity: Make a Meaningful Frame/Mat

You may wish to frame/mat your Bible People Portraits in a way that is symbolic of the person whose portrait you are framing.

Some examples:

- **Abraham**—He traveled to many places, including across deserts. Cover a frame with glue and sprinkle sand over it.

- **Esau**—You might glue uncooked lentil beans to the frame, representing Esau giving up his birthright for a bowl of lentil stew.

- **Jacob**—Draw ladders around the frame, representing Jacob's ladder.

- **Joseph**—Use markers to make multicolored stripes around the frame, representing Joseph's robe (although we know it was a robe of long sleeves, not necessarily a robe of many colors).

- **Moses**—Draw Roman numerals I through X around the frame, one for each of the Ten Commandments.

- **King David or Queen Esther**—Draw outlines of crowns, then fill them in with glue. Cover crowns with glitter and plastic "jewels" from the craft store to represent royalty.

- **Jesus**—Write names for Jesus (see page 93) on the frame, using glitter pens.

- **John the Baptist**—Glue scalloped shells onto the frame. The scalloped shell is the symbol for John the Baptist. The scalloped shell with three drops of water added is the Christian symbol for baptism.

- **Judas Iscariot**—Make his frame look broken or lopsided. Cover it with thin threads of cotton batting, making them look like cobwebs.

- **Zacchaeus**—Glue coins to the frame to represent the tax collector's profession.

- **Paul**—Use brilliant colored paints to make an abstract representation of the blinding light Paul saw on the road to Damascus.

- Write words on frames surrounding a piece of art. They may be words of faith, or you can use a Bible verse that relates to specific biblical people.

ESAU   *Some say his name means* **hairy** *or* **red** *as he is described in the Bible, but the meaning is not really clear. Esau was born before his twin brother, Jacob.*

Esau was Isaac's favorite son. But before his birth it was known he would be secondary to Jacob. Esau's mother favored his brother over Esau and was upset with Esau's marriages to foreign wives, which made for difficult family relationships (Genesis 26:34-35; 27:46).

Esau was a hunter and sometimes impulsive. Esau sold his birthright to Jacob for a meal of lentil stew and bread (Genesis 25:29-34).

When his birthright was stolen by his brother with the help of his mother, Esau was understandably very angry. However, when Jacob asked forgiveness, Esau forgave him. After the reconciliation of the brothers, Esau does not appear in the biblical account until the death of Isaac. Esau and Jacob together buried their father (Genesis 35:29).

RACHEL   *(meaning* **ewe***) Rachel was Jacob's second wife, his true love, and the younger daughter of Laban. This made her Jacob's cousin.*

Rachel was a shepherdess. Jacob fell in love with her the first time he saw her and worked fourteen years to marry her. When they left Laban's house, Rachel stole the household gods.

Though she was Jacob's favorite wife, she was jealous of Leah because Leah produced many children, all but one sons. Finally, God blessed Rachel and she became the mother of Joseph and Benjamin.

LEAH   *(meaning* **cow***) Jacob's first wife, elder daughter of Laban. This made her Jacob's cousin.*

A rival of Rachel's for her husband's affection, Leah was not Jacob's first choice. Laban tricked Jacob into marrying her.

Leah was the mother of six of Jacob's sons—Reuben, Simeon, Levi, Judah, Issachar, Zebulun—and Jacob's only daughter, Dinah. Though Jacob loved Rachel best, it was Leah who was an ancestor of David, the great king.

Leah also gave Jacob her maid Bilhah, who bore Jacob two sons, and her maid Zilpah, who also bore him two sons.

Rachel and Leah are treated equally in Ruth 4:11, where it is noted that they "together built up the house of Israel." Leah deserves an honored place in Israel's history.

Activity: Make Fun Frames/Mats

You may wish to frame your Bible People Portraits in fun and unusual ways. Below are just a few examples of possible ways you may wish to decorate frames.

• **Make a scented frame.** Cut two pieces of cloth, each of a size to fit as a frame around the art. Sew or staple the pieces to the mat for the art, leaving an opening so that it can be stuffed. Stuff your frame with potpourri (or with cotton or felt soaked in perfume). Staple or sew shut.

• **Spatter paint a frame.** Try using a fan brush. Have participants place the fan brush soaked in paint against the side of their hand and then push it forward across the frame. This type of spatter painting makes it easier to control where the paint will spatter. This method of spatter painting works best with fifth graders and up. Younger children may not have the proper motor skills to do this well. If you have younger children, let them use the traditional spatter painting techniques.

• **Glue unusual items to your frames.** Use straw, cotton balls, plastic knives and forks, twigs, buttons, dried flowers, or rolling eyes from craft stores. Anything your imagination can come up with and that can be held by glue can be used for making frames.

• **Use precut foam pieces.** These have a sticky backing for attaching them to frames. You can find them in many religious shapes.

• **Make potato stamps.** Cut the ends of potatoes into designs, making a stamp. Press the potatoes into colored ink pads and then stamp the frames.

• **Buy colorful birthday candles.** Light the candles and let participants carefully drip the melting wax onto a posterboard or art paper frame. CAUTION: THIS METHOD TAKES A LOT OF ADULT SUPERVISION. Have a bucket of water handy in case someone gets the candle too close to the paper!

• **Make "Wanted" posters.** Instead of framing in the usual manner, make "wanted" type posters out of the Bible People Portraits. Have participants come up with clever ways to state what each person is "wanted" for.

JOSEPH *(meaning* **may God add***) It is Joseph's story that sets the stage for the rest of Israel's history. It is through Joseph that the Hebrews end up in Egypt and eventually fall into slavery. This slavery ends through deliverance in the form of Moses.*

At the age of 17, Joseph was a tattletale (Genesis 37:2), more than a little spoiled, and much loved by Jacob as the son of his old age (Genesis 37:3). Joseph was given a special gift of a robe with long sleeves which might have had some connotation of royalty, but at the least made working more difficult (Genesis 37:3). To make matters worse, Joseph kept having dreams that he told his brothers about, dreams where they bowed down to him. This pushed ten of his brothers over the edge (Benjamin, his younger brother, was not involved), and they decided to get rid of him. Like all brothers, they didn't completely agree on the plan. Some wanted to kill him; Reuben, the oldest, wanted to put him in a well; Judah came up with the final plan—selling him off.

Ironically, while the brothers of Joseph tried to change the outcome of his dreams of superiority, they inadvertently set up the context in which the predicted events could occur. Joseph was sold into Egypt, where he did well until he was falsely accused of making advances to Potiphar's wife and was thrown into prison. He was let out of prison because of his ability to interpret dreams. The interpretation of the pharaoh's dreams of feast and famine led the pharaoh to set Joseph over the preparation for the famine, which is what finally united his family and resulted in their move to Egypt.

Outline of Joseph's Story

• Joseph is born (Genesis 30:22-24).

• At 17 Joseph has two dreams that he tells his brothers. In both dreams they are bowing down to him. In the second dream his mother and father bow to him also. This angers his brothers (Genesis 37:5-11).

• Joseph is sold and taken to Egypt, where he is bought by Potiphar (captain of the guard for the pharaoh). He becomes an overseer in Potiphar's household (Genesis 37:12-36; 39:1-6).

• Joseph is very good looking. Potiphar's wife falsely accuses him of attacking her when Joseph refuses her advances (Genesis 39).

• Joseph is sent to prison, where he interprets the dreams of two prisoners (Genesis 40).

• Two years later Joseph is asked to interpret Pharaoh's dreams. Joseph says the dreams mean that there will be seven good years and seven lean years. Joseph rises to power (Genesis 41).

• Joseph's brothers come to Egypt because of the famine. Joseph recognizes them and insists that they go back to Canaan and return with his brother Benjamin (Genesis 42).

• The brothers return to Egypt with Benjamin where Joseph keeps him. Joseph finally reveals himself to his brothers (Genesis 43–45).

• Joseph's entire family moves to Egypt (Genesis 46–47).

• Jacob blesses Joseph's sons (Genesis 48).

• Joseph forgives his brothers (Genesis 50:15-21).

• Joseph dies at age 110 and is buried in Egypt (Genesis 50:26).

Activity: Food Service Project

Joseph helped the Egyptians prepare for a famine, and because of this the Egyptians and many of their neighbors (including Joseph's family) did not starve.

When studying Joseph or a story that deals with food/hunger (such as Jesus feeding the five thousand or Ruth gleaning in Boaz's fields), incorporate a food service project with the study.

Possible Food Service Projects:

• Together plan, prepare, and serve a meal at Room in the Inn (or at a soup kitchen). After serving, all participants mingle among the homeless and eat with them, sharing fellowship as well as food.

• Have a canned goods drive for the local Second Harvest Food Bank.

• In the summer have people bring extra vegetables from their gardens to share with other members of the congregation.

• If there is a family in the congregation in need, have participants collect money and purchase a gift certificate to the local supermarket. Have it given anonymously through the pastor to the family. (A family might not want the entire congregation to know they are having difficulties. You might ask the pastor if there is such a family without getting the name or details, thereby preserving the family's right to privacy.)

• Together bake cookies, place them in attractive baskets or boxes, and deliver them to shut-ins and those in nursing homes. Divide up the distribution with each pair/team planning to spend a few minutes visiting with the cookie recipient.

• Have several families work together to provide a meal for the entire congregation. This could be a fundraiser for the local food bank or another special mission project. It also provides good quality time for families.

• Get together on Saturday and make Sunday morning snacks for the entire Sunday school—children, youth, and adults. You will also have to be prepared to do the distribution on Sunday morning. Avoid the temptation to purchase the snacks; it is in the baking and serving that truly valuable memories will be made, and young adolescents get the chance to serve. Serving others builds character.

Old Testament Leaders

Activity: Wilderness Challenge

Divide participants into small groups. Give each group a photocopy of the challenge below. Tell them that they will have twenty minutes to come up with solutions to the challenge posed. Unlike popular television "reality" shows, they will not have special "games" or tricks thrown at them. They will only have to decide how to cope with the challenge.

After the challenge has been completed, bring all of the groups back together, share decisions, and look at the following Scriptures to see how the Hebrews (or Moses) dealt with these challenges while wandering forty years in the wilderness.

Exodus

Water: Exodus 15:22-27. The people complain. Moses turns to God. Bitter water is made sweet.
Water: Exodus 17:1-7. The people complain. Moses turns to God. Water is brought from a rock.
Food: Exodus 16. The people complain. Moses turns to God. God provides manna and quail. (May use just verses 2-3, 11-15, 31, and 35.)
Boredom (and Fear): Exodus 32. The Golden Calf. The people get tired of waiting and turn from God. Moses pleads for God to forgive the people.
Fear: All of the above. The people complain and wish they were back in Egypt where they were slaves. Moses turns to God.

You are a group of people lost in a mountainous region with little natural vegetation, but there are wild animals in the area. You have been wandering around lost for several weeks without coming across anyone. You have no modern technological equipment (no cell phones, computers, GPS, and so forth). No one has a compass or a map. You have no food or water left.

You do have tents, sleeping bags, matches, warm clothes, and cooking utensils.

How do you solve these problems?

1. Water   3. Boredom

2. Food   4. Fear

MOSES

Some scholars say the name is Egyptian and means **is son**; *others say that it comes from Hebrew and means* **pulled** *or* **drawn out of**.

You might use any or all of these titles to describe Moses:

> *founder of the Jewish faith*
> *great liberator*
> *lawgiver*
> *prophet*

Founder of the Jewish faith: *While it was Abraham who first made a covenant to follow only one God, it was Moses who led the people into a formal relationship with God.*

Great Liberator: *It was Moses who brought the Israelites out of the land of Egypt and led them to the Promised Land of Canaan, though he never entered the Promised Land himself.*

Lawgiver: *It was Moses who gave the Israelites their code of law, including the moral laws by which people were to live their daily lives. Moses made it clear he was not of the same status as God (not unheard of for leaders in biblical times), but rather God's spokesman, receiving God's will for the people and bringing it to them.*

Prophet: *A biblical prophet is one who carries messages from God to the people. And Moses intercedes with God on behalf of the people (Exodus 32:31-32; 33:12-23).*

Moses as a person was very complex. Put in a basket in the Nile as an infant to be saved from the pharaoh, he lived as the son of Pharaoh's daughter but was raised by his own mother. He was raised in a life of privilege.

As a young man Moses got into serious trouble. He killed an Egyptian he saw beating a Hebrew slave. He knew what he did was wrong because he hid the body. (In fact, because it was an Egyptian he killed, the crime could have been considered a crime against the pharaoh.) The very next day he lost his temper with two Hebrews who were fighting. They let it be known that they knew of his crime. Moses fled to Midian. He no sooner got there than he came to the defense of the priests's seven daughters when shepherds tried to keep them from watering their flocks. As a reward he was allowed to marry Zipporah, one of the priest's daughters. All of this took only half of Exodus Chapter 2! Moses didn't like social injustice, but as a young man he did not always make wise choices in how to deal with it.

Many reasons are given for why Moses did not live to enter the Promised Land. Two of the reasons often stated are that 1) Moses did not properly recognize God (Deuteronomy 32:48-52), or 2) because of the sins of the people (Deuteronomy 1:34-45; 3:18-28).

- Pharaoh asks midwives to the Hebrew women in Egypt to kill all boy babies. The midwives will not do this because they fear God. Pharaoh then commands that every Hebrew boy baby is to be thrown into the Nile River (Exodus 1:15-22).

- Moses is born in Egypt. His mother hides him in bulrushes with his sister Miriam to look over him. He is discovered and raised by Pharaoh's daughter, though his own mother becomes his nurse (Exodus 2:1-10).

- Moses kills an Egyptian who was beating an Israelite slave, interferes with a quarrel between two Hebrews, and flees to Midian. In Midian he defends the seven daughters of the priest and marries one of them, Zipporah (Exodus 2:11-24).

- Moses hears God calling him from a bush that was burning, but not consumed. Moses protests, but finally agrees to go when God sends Moses' brother, Aaron, with him (Exodus 3-4).

- Moses returns to Egypt and asks the pharaoh to let the Hebrews go into the wilderness to celebrate a festival. Pharaoh answers by making the work of the Hebrews harder (Exodus 5).

- God commands Moses again to go to Pharaoh. Moses protests that he is a poor speaker. God says Aaron can speak for Moses. Moses is 80 years old and Aaron 83 (Exodus 6:28–7:7).

- Aaron throws down his staff before Pharaoh, and it becomes a snake (Exodus 7:8-13).

- Nine times Moses goes to Pharaoh and nine plagues are brought on Egypt, but Pharaoh refuses to let the Israelites go (Exodus 7:14–10:29).

- Warning of the final plague—death of the firstborn of Egypt (Exodus 11).

- First Passover is instituted (Exodus 12:1-28).

- The tenth plague—death of the firstborn. Pharaoh summons Moses and tells him to take the Israelites and leave (Exodus 12:29-42).

- The Exodus from Egypt (Exodus 12:33–15:27).

The following events take place during the forty years of wandering in the wilderness:

- The people complain they are hungry. They are given bread from heaven (Exodus 16).

- The people complain they have no water. Moses at God's command brings water from the rock (Exodus 17:1-7).

- Israel defeats Amalek (Exodus 17:8-16).

- Moses follows Jethro's advice to appoint able men to help him lead the people (Exodus 18).

- The Israelites reach Mount Sinai. Moses is summoned by the Lord to the top of the mountain (Exodus 19).

- Moses is given the Ten Commandments (Exodus 20) and the conquest of Canaan is promised (Exodus 23:20-33). Moses is on the mountain forty days and forty nights (Exodus 24:18). During this time Moses also receives detailed instructions for constructing the tabernacle (Exodus 25:1–31:17).

- Moses smashes the first tablets of the Law when he returns to the camp to discover Aaron has helped the people build a golden calf (Exodus 32:19).

- Moses begs God to spare the Israelites from God's anger (Exodus 32:31–33:23).

- Moses makes new tablets and the covenant is renewed (Exodus 34). This takes another forty days and forty nights (Exodus 34:28).

- Moses takes a census (Numbers 1:1-2).

- In the fortieth year, on the first day of the eleventh month after the Exodus, Moses speaks to the people, recalling their journey and warning them not to forget God (Deuteronomy 1:1–4:40).

- Moses' death foretold (Deuteronomy 32:48-52).

- Moses' final blessing on Israel (Deuteronomy 33).

- Moses dies at 120 years of age and is buried in Moab (Deuteronomy 34).

MIRIAM *(derived from **Mary**) Sister to Moses and Aaron.*

Miriam watched over Moses when he was placed in a basket among the reeds, and she offered to bring a nurse for the child. The nurse, of course, was her mother (Exodus 2:2-8).

Miriam was a prophet (Exodus 15:20). It is obvious that Miriam was with Aaron and Moses in Egypt, as it was Miriam who led the women in singing and dancing in victory after the crossing of the Red Sea (Exodus 15:20-21).

Miriam and Aaron became jealous of Moses and criticized Moses' leadership as well as his marriage to an Ethiopian (Numbers 12). Though God was angry with both Aaron and Miriam, it was only Miriam who was actually punished. We do not know why. But her skin turned white from a skin disease that some say was leprosy; others say it could have been a different disease. Aaron asked Moses to help, so Moses asked God to heal Miriam. Because of this, Miriam's disease lasted only seven days (Numbers 12:10-15).

The Bible does not say whether she was married, but there is a rabbinical tradition that she was a wife and mother. Miriam died at Kadesh and was buried there (Numbers 20:1). Micah 6:4 claims her as one of leaders of the Exodus.

AARON *Brother of Moses. He was three years older than Moses*

(Exodus 7:7). Aaron was sent by God with Moses to Egypt. He is called Moses' "prophet" (Exodus 7:1). Moses was to speak what God said, but it was Aaron who was to tell Pharaoh, "Let the Israelites go" (Exodus 7:2). Aaron's staff was thrown down in front of Pharaoh and became a snake. When the staff was used, God instructed Moses to have Aaron use it (Exodus 7:19). It is known as the staff of Aaron (Exodus 7:12).

Aaron was the first priest of Israel. This role was so important that even how he was to be dressed was described in the Bible (Exodus 28). Aaron was a Levite, and it is from Aaron that the line of priests is traced.

It was Aaron who helped the people of Israel make a golden idol out of their jewelry. This act of disobedience ended in God's bringing a plague on the Israelites (Exodus 32).

Like Moses and Miriam, Aaron was not to enter the Promised Land. He died and was buried on Mount Hor. He was mourned by the house of Israel for thirty days (Numbers 20:22-29).

Activity: Playing with Sevens

Dealing with a biblical story such as the seven days of Creation, Joshua and the battle of Jericho, or the Acts story of the seven chosen to serve the church? You might wish to introduce the importance of the number seven (it is prominent in many biblical stories; see page 42) with some games or activities that center on the number seven. Try one of these ideas:

- Divide the participants into seven pairs or groups (or, if a very large group, divide them into teams of seven people each). Assign whatever activity, questions, or biblical study to be done in these groups.

- As in the above description, divide participants into groups. Give each group a list of seven things or tasks to perform. For example:

    LISTS:

    Look up seven Bible verses.
    Make a list of seven ways people can follow Jesus.
    Make a list of seven spiritual disciplines.

    OR
    TASKS:

    Task 1: Set up a place in the room for worship.
    Task 2: Prepare an opening prayer.
    Task 3: Decide on a Bible verse to read for worship.
    Task 4: Practice singing a song to lead in worship.
    Task 5: Find matches to light the candles.
    Task 6: Write a closing prayer.
    Task 7: Divide up parts of the worship service among your group members.

- Bring in seven objects and see how many of them each person can juggle.

- Make up a "Jericho" parade. Have participants make an "ark" from a cardboard box (cover with gold wrapping paper, punch holes, and run dowel rods through two sides of the box so it can be carried, make "trumpets" from rolled up newspaper). Have seven participants march seven times around the room with some of them carrying the ark. Then have them blow their trumpets seven times. (Or you could divide up the two tasks.)

JOSHUA *(meaning* **Yahweh saves** *or* **Yahweh is salvation***) Successor to Moses. Joshua leads the Israelites into the Promised Land.*

At the time of the Exodus, Joshua was a young man and an assistant to Moses (Exodus 33:11). Early in the Exodus it was Joshua who led the Israelites in the defeat of Amalek (Exodus 17:13).

Joshua was sent with Caleb and ten others into Canaan to see what they would be facing. Ten spies brought back reports filled with doubts and fears. But Caleb and Joshua brought a favorable report. Because of this Caleb and Joshua were the only two adults that left Egypt to be allowed into the Promised Land (Numbers 14:24 and Deuteronomy 1:35-38).

Before Moses died, Joshua was commissioned to be his successor. Joshua led the people into the Promised Land. It was Joshua who acted as the transition character from exile to homeland. Joshua's role was pivotal for the Israelites, and a good portion of his story is the detailing of the conquering and settling of Canaan.

RAHAB *Rahab was a prostitute in Jericho. Looking at the world at the time, she was probably a prostitute in order to help her poor family survive.*

God had a special role for Rahab to play. She hid from the king the two spies sent by Joshua, and in return she and her family were spared (Joshua 2). She is remembered in Hebrews 11:31 in a list of heroes of the faith.

Outline of Joshua's Story

- Joshua, a young warrior, helps defeat an attack by Amelek (Exodus 17:13).

- Young Joshua leaves Egypt with the Exodus and is an assistant to Moses. He goes with Moses to the mountain of God (Exodus 24:13).

- Joshua warns Moses there is a noise in the Israelite camp at the time of the celebration of the golden calf (Exodus 32:17).

- Joshua and Caleb are sent with others into Jericho to spy on the land. They are the only two to bring back good reports. God rewards them by promising they will live to enter the Promised Land (Numbers 13:1–14:24; Deuteronomy 1:35-38).

- Joshua is commissioned to be Moses' successor (Deuteronomy 31).

- Joshua takes over at the death of Moses (Deuteronomy 34:9).

- God gives Joshua instructions on how to enter and take over the Promised Land (Joshua 1).

- Joshua sends spies into Jericho (Joshua 2).

- Priests carrying the ark lead the people across the Jordan. Twelve stones are set up in remembrance (Joshua 3:1–4:24).

- Jericho is taken and destroyed (Joshua 6).

- Joshua fights many battles to conquer the Promised Land (Joshua 7–12).

- Joshua divides up the land among the twelve tribes of Israel (Joshua 13–22).

- Joshua gives a farewell address to the Israelites, warning them not to forget God (Joshua 23).

- Joshua gathers the tribes and they renew their covenant with God (Joshua 24:1-28).

- Joshua dies at the age of 110. He is buried in Ephraim (Joshua 24:29-30).

Activity: It's a Puzzle

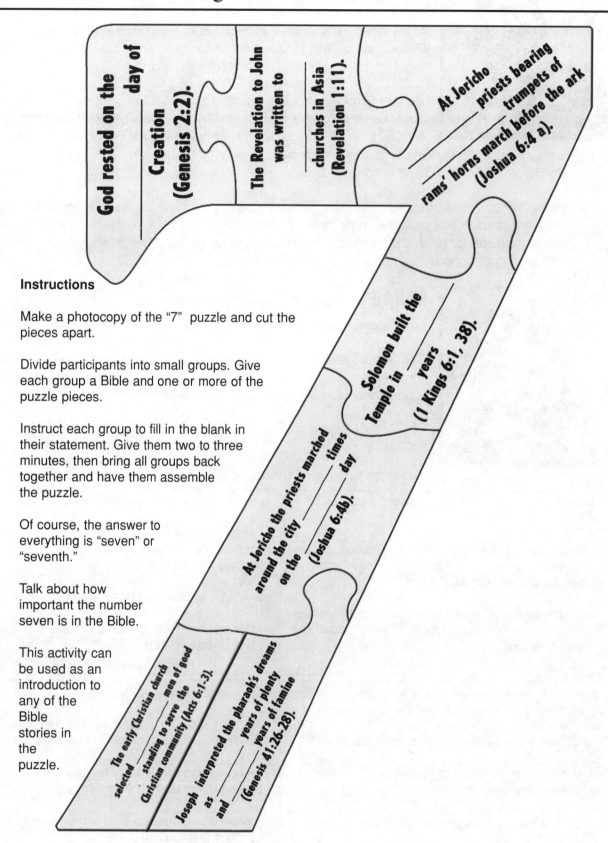

God rested on the _____ day of Creation (Genesis 2:2).

The Revelation to John was written to _____ churches in Asia (Revelation 1:11).

At Jericho _____ priests bearing trumpets of rams' horns march before the ark (Joshua 6:4 a).

Solomon built the Temple in _____ years (1 Kings 6:1, 38).

At Jericho the priests marched around the city _____ times on the _____ day (Joshua 6:4b).

The early Christian church selected _____ men of good standing to serve the Christian community (Acts 6:1-3).

Joseph interpreted the pharaoh's dreams as _____ years of plenty and _____ years of famine (Genesis 41:26-28).

Instructions

Make a photocopy of the "7" puzzle and cut the pieces apart.

Divide participants into small groups. Give each group a Bible and one or more of the puzzle pieces.

Instruct each group to fill in the blank in their statement. Give them two to three minutes, then bring all groups back together and have them assemble the puzzle.

Of course, the answer to everything is "seven" or "seventh."

Talk about how important the number seven is in the Bible.

This activity can be used as an introduction to any of the Bible stories in the puzzle.

JUDGES

Between the time of Joshua and Saul, Israel had no formal central leader. Into this leadership vacuum stepped the judges. Judges arose when the stability of Israel was threatened. Judges were probably local military rulers.

DEBORAH *(meaning* **bee***) Deborah was the fourth judge of Israel. She was also a prophetess and a military leader. Deborah was the only judge who actually settled disputes. Her story is told in Judges 4-5.*

Deborah told Barak that God called him to fight a general, Sisera. Barak insisted that Deborah go with him into the battle. Deborah and Barak led the assault together.

Deborah's song of victory is considered one of the oldest passages in the Bible.

GIDEON *The fifth judge of Israel. His story is told in Judges 6–8. He is also called* **Jerubbaal** *(Judges 6:32).*

Gideon destroyed his family's idols (Judges 6:28-35), used a fleece of wool to determine God's will (Judges 6:36-40), and defeated an army of Midianites with 300 soldiers (Judges 7).

The last part of Gideon's story is marred because he refused the kingship offered by the people. They then set up a substitute (an ephod) and the Israelites begin to worship it as an idol (a god) (Judges 8).

SAMSON *Unlike the other judges, Samson was not a military leader. Rather, he waged his war on the Philistines as an individual. Samson was dedicated as a nazirite by his mother. Nazirites were to let their hair grow long, to avoid any form of strong drink, and to eat only clean food.*

Samson was a man who strove single-handedly against the Philistines. He is best known for his more-than-human strength. The source of his strength was in his hair. Samson's contribution to Israel was its continued survival because of the number of Philistines he killed.

Samson fell in love with a beautiful Philistine woman named Delilah, who tricked him into telling her the source of his strength. When she discovered it was his hair, she had his hair shaved off as he slept. He was taken off to prison by the Philistines. During his imprisonment his hair began to grow again (Judges 16:22). Samson was brought into a gathering of 3000 Philistines who had come to see him perform. He prayed to God for strength and died along with the Philistines when he managed to push down the two supporting pillars of the house. See Judges 13–16.

Bible People of Faith

Activity: Create Your Own Country

This activity would be a good exercise when studying Israel's entry into the Promised Land after the Exodus. It would relate well to the time of the judges, but would be even more appropriate for when the Israelites called for a king, wanting to be like other countries around them (1 Samuel 8). Up to this point Israel had been a loose confederation of tribes.

This activity may be done with all participants working together, or for large groups, with participants divided into smaller groups, each group creating its own country.

You will need: Reproducbiles on pages 46 and 48, pencils, and Bibles
     Optional: large sheets of newsprint and markers

Instructions: The participants or group of participants will be given thirty minutes to form a country using the two reproducibles on pages 46 and 48. They will be allowed to use their Bibles. Refer them either to the Book of Judges or to 1 Samuel 8.

The group or groups will need to fill out completely the two reproducibles. Help them understand the section on what the country stands for by having them think about what are the things they all believe are most important *(For example: life, liberty, the pursuit of happiness; freedom, equality, and harmony; righteous living; worship on Sundays; happy childhoods; and so forth).* When making ten laws, encourage them not to just say "the Ten Commandments," but to really think about the issues. After all, the most important law for Christians is the Golden Rule (Matthew 7:12). If participants do decide to use the Ten Commandments, they need to restate them in terms of problems that might face their country.

• If you do this as one group, you will not need to use follow-up discussion of the issues, as the discussion will take place while you are making decisions.

• If you do this exercise in small groups, bring the groups back together and have each group report back what some of the issues were that came up in their decision making. What was the biggest issue?

For either process follow up with a discussion of the biblical story that you are using as the basis.

Ask questions, such as why did Israel continue to get in trouble? *(They constantly had trouble whether they had a judge or a king because they began to stray from the Word of God. Their neighbors and their daily wants and cares took over, and they were easily led to other gods or to neglecting their relationship with God.)*

SAMUEL *Son of Elkanah and Hannah. Hannah prayed to God for a child and promised to dedicate him as a nazirite (see Numbers 6:1-21 for details on nazirites) if God granted her wish. Samuel was born, was dedicated as a nazirite, and left in the care of Eli the priest as promised.*

As a child, Samuel was called by God to commit himself to God. A previous commitment was made for him by his mother, but Samuel himself responded when called.

Samuel is a transitional figure in Israel's history. Acts 3:24 and Acts 13:20 see Samuel as the first of the prophets. First Samuel 7 shows Samuel in his role as the last great judge. Samuel also filled some priestly functions. Like Deborah, Samuel acted as a judge in settling disputes. Israel was in trouble. Even the judges and priests were beginning to stray from God. And Israel was under attack from neighbors.

Samuel's greatest contribution to Israel was his anointing of Saul as king, and then his later rejection of Saul and anointing of David as Saul's successor to the throne. It appears in First Samuel 8 that Samuel was opposed to the people having a king, knowing that kings bring armies, taxes, and other problems. But God told Samuel to anoint a king, so he did.

Eventually, with Saul's descent into madness, Samuel was forced to anoint a new king. Before Saul's death, Samuel anointed David king. With Samuel the story of a loose confederation of tribes gives way to Israel's greatest days as a nation united under a monarchy.

Outline of Samuel's Story

- Samuel is born to Hannah, who dedicates him to the Lord as "long as he lives." He is taken to the temple and put in the care of the priest Eli (1 Samuel 1).

- Samuel as a young boy is called by God. He prophesies the destruction of Eli's sons (1 Samuel 3).

- Samuel gathers the people of Israel and begins his work as judge (1 Samuel 7). As judge Samuel has a circuit where he goes year by year to judge Israel (1 Samuel 7:15-16).

- Israel demands a king and Samuel objects (1 Samuel 8:1-18).

- Israel's demand for a king is granted (1 Samuel 8:19-22).

- It is revealed to Samuel that God has chosen Saul to be king, and Samuel anoints Saul (1 Samuel 9–10).

- Samuel makes a farewell address to Israel (1 Samuel 12).

- Samuel arrives late at Gilgal. Saul gets tired of waiting and makes an unlawful sacrifice. Samuel rebukes him (1 Samuel 13:1-14).

- Saul defeats the Amalekites but does not carry out Samuel's instructions from God (1 Samuel 15:1-9).

- Samuel informs Saul that he has been rejected as king (1 Samuel 15:10-35).

- Samuel anoints Jesse's son David as king (1 Samuel 16:1-13).

- Samuel dies and is buried in Ramah (1 Samuel 25:1).

Activity: Our Country

_____
(Name of Country)

The three things our country stands for:

_____

_____

_____

Form of government _____
(democracy, benign dictatorship, republic, anarchy, and so forth)

Leadership   _____

_____

_____

_____

How our country will defend itself_____

SAUL

*[meaning **asked** (of God)] First king of Israel. Ruled from about 1020 to 1000 B.C. Son of Kish from the tribe of Benjamin.*

Though often seen as a bad man, Saul is probably one of those transition characters that has no blueprint and therefore cannot last, but makes the next stage possible. His story is told in 1 Samuel 8–31.

Saul was chosen by God and anointed by Samuel to be the first king of Israel. Saul was a very capable military leader, and it was due to his battles with the Philistines that David was able to make Israel a nation (1 Samuel).

Almost immediately Saul's relationship with Samuel began to deteriorate. It appears that Saul's mental health began to deteriorate also. Or perhaps he was just trying to cope with the multiple problems around him—quarreling Israelites, neighbors trying to destroy Israel, and Samuel, who attempted to keep Israel's relationship with God at the center of life and decisions.

Saul was twice rejected for his actions. First, Saul got impatient waiting for Samuel to arrive at Gilgal and to make a burnt offering to God, so Saul made it. This was an affront to the priestly duty of Samuel. After Saul defeated the Amalekites, Saul spared the king, which was against what God had commanded.

Saul was jealous of David and tried to kill him. He married his daughter Michal to David as part of a plot, but she helped David escape. Saul's son Jonathan remained David's loyal friend.

When the Philistines killed Saul's sons in battle, Saul committed suicide by falling on his sword.

Outline of Saul's Story

- Saul is chosen, anointed by Samuel, and proclaimed the first king of Israel (1 Samuel 9–10).

- Saul defeats the Ammonites (1 Samuel 11).

- Saul makes an unlawful sacrifice (1 Samuel 13).

- Saul makes a rash oath that almost costs his son Jonathan his life (1 Samuel 14:24-46).

- Saul defeats the Amalekites, but spares their king. Because of this, God withdraws his favor and Saul is rejected as king (1 Samuel 15).

- Saul is tormented by an evil spirit. David is brought to him to play the lyre and to soothe him (1 Samuel 16:14-23).

- David, the young shepherd boy, slays the giant Philistine, Goliath. David becomes Jonathan's instant friend, and Saul becomes jealous and throws a spear at David twice. Saul becomes afraid of David and makes him a commander (1 Samuel 17:1–18:16).

- Saul gives his daughter to David in marriage in hopes of distracting him and perhaps making him become careless (1 Samuel 18:17-30).

- Saul's son and daughter save David (1 Samuel 19).

- Saul slaughters the priests at Nob for conspiring with David (1 Samuel 22:6-23).

- Saul takes three thousand men to look for David. When David has a chance to kill Saul, he instead spares Saul's life (1 Samuel 24).

- David spares Saul's life a second time (1 Samuel 26).

- Saul consults a medium, trying to contact the ghost of Samuel (1 Samuel 28).

- Saul's sons are killed in battle, and Saul kills himself by falling on his own sword (1 Samuel 31).

Activity: Law Code

We hereby decree that we, the citizens of _____ , will live by the
ten laws in our law code.   (Name of Country)

1. _____

2. _____

3. _____

4. _____

5. _____

6. _____

7. _____

8. _____

9. _____

10. _____

How laws will be enforced: _____

Bible People of Faith

DAVID *The great king of Israel. The youngest of Jesse's sons (1 Samuel 16:11-13). David was brought before Samuel and anointed king of Israel. He did not actually ascend to the throne until the death of Saul many years later.*

David was the great warrior king who united the kingdom. He brought the ark into Jerusalem.

He had many wives and many children. Of his wives Michal (Saul's daughter), Abigail (widow of Nabal), and Bathsheba (widow of Uriah) are important parts of David's story.

Known for greatness in battle and in administration, David let the sins of his personal life spill over into the life of the nation. This led to a struggle among his sons for control of the kingdom. David almost waited too long to name his successor, and a rebellion took place.

David is the symbol of the messianic hopes of Israel. Jews await the day that a king from the line of David will rule. Christians trace the genealogy of Jesus from the "stump of Jesse," the house of David. (See genealogy on pages 84-85.)

Outline of David's Story

- Young David is anointed king by Samuel (1 Samuel 16:1-13).

- David plays the lyre to soothe king Saul (1 Samuel 16:14-23).

- David kills the Philistine giant, Goliath (1 Samuel 17).

- Jonathan makes a covenant with David (1 Samuel 18:1-5).

- Saul tries to kill David with a spear (1 Samuel 18:10-16).

- David marries Michal, and Jonathan and Michal help David escape from Saul (1 Samuel 19).

- David has a chance to kill Saul, but spares him (1 Samuel 24).

- When refused food, David prepares to attack Nabal. Abigail stops David and negotiates peace. Ten days later Nabal dies, and David marries Abigail (1 Samuel 25).

- David spares Saul's life a second time (1 Samuel 26).

- The Philistines reject David (1 Samuel 29).

- David mourns Saul and Jonathan (2 Samuel 1).

- David is anointed King of Judah (2 Samuel 2:1-7).

- Abner deserts the house of Saul and joins David (2 Samuel 3).

- David is anointed king of all Israel and unites the kingdom (2 Samuel 5).

- David brings the ark to Jerusalem (2 Samuel 6).

- God makes a covenant with David (2 Samuel 7).

- David commits adultery with Bathsheba and orders the murder of Uriah. David marries Bathsheba. Nathan rebukes David. David and Bathsheba's first child dies. Solomon, their son, is born (2 Samuel 11–12).

- Problems arise among David's children. His son Absalom rebels. David is forced to flee Jerusalem (2 Samuel 13–15).

- Absalom is defeated. David grieves (2 Samuel 18–19).

- David angers the Lord by ordering a census, and the Lord lets David choose from three options for punishment for his sins (2 Samuel 24).

- David finally chooses Solomon as the next king and gives instructions to Solomon (1 Kings 1–2).

- David dies. He had reigned forty years (1 Kings 2:10).

JONATHAN *(meaning* **Yahweh has given***) Jonathan was the son of Saul, friend of David, and father of Mephibosheth.*

Jonathan was a great warrior and helped his father defeat the Philistines in battle (example: 1 Samuel 14). Jonathan was loyal to his father, to his friend David, and to God. Jonathan tried to bring Saul and David together, but when he realized that Saul really was intent on killing David, he helped David escape (1 Samuel 20).

Jonathan continued to fight in his father's army. He was killed along with his brothers when they were defeated by the Philistines in battle (1 Samuel 31).

MEPHIBOSHETH *(originally* **Meribbaal***, 1 Chronicles 8:34, but was changed to disguise the portion of his name that was related to the ancient god Baal)*

Mephibosheth, the son of Jonathan, was only five years old when Jonathan was killed. In her haste to flee with the boy, his nurse dropped him and this caused his lameness (2 Samuel 4:4).

Mephibosheth was taken in by David (probably so he could keep an eye on Saul's heir). Jonathan's inheritance was split between him and Ziba (a steward in Saul's household) when David could not decide which one had been loyal and which had been a traitor during a rebellion (2 Samuel 19:24-30).

ABSALOM *The third son of David. He was very handsome.*

To avenge the rape of his sister, Absalom arranged for the murder of Amnon (his half-brother) and was forced to flee (2 Samuel 13). He was later reconciled with his father (2 Samuel 14).

It is through Absalom that David suffered the consequences of his sins of adultery with Bathsheba and murder of Uriah (2 Samuel 11:1–12:15). Solomon was born to David and Bathsheba. He was younger than Absalom.

When David waited too long to announce a successor to his throne, Absalom led a rebellion, trying to take the throne. Absalom was finally defeated and killed.

Absalom's rebellion and death broke David's heart (2 Samuel 18).

Like the story of Samson, the story of Absalom is not appropriate for young children. One message of Absalom's story is that sin has consequences, often far beyond what we can anticipate.

ABIGAIL

ABIGAIL *(may mean* **my father is joy***)* *Wife of Nabal and then David's second wife. Mother of David's second-born son, Chileab (2 Samuel 3:3).*

Abigail was married to Nabal (meaning **fool***). Nabal refused to give food to David's men when they asked for it. David became angry and prepared to attack Nabal. Abigail intervened, supplied David and his men with food, and begged him to spare Nabal. David blessed her for stopping him (1 Samuel 25).*

About ten days later Nabal died. Abigail married David.

Abigail and another of David's wives are taken captive by the Amalekites (1 Samuel 30:5). They are rescued, and Abigail goes with him to Hebron when David is anointed king.

BATHSHEBA *(meaning* **daughter of abundance***) Wife of Uriah and then wife of David. Mother of Solomon.*

King David seduced Bathsheba and then had her husband, Uriah, set up to be killed in battle. There is nothing that says Bathsheba knew anything about this plan (2 Samuel 11).

Towards the end of David's life, the prophet Nathan and Bathsheba worked together to have Solomon succeed his father as king of Israel (1 Kings 1:11-31).

NATHAN *A prophet to both David and his son Solomon.*

Nathan first appears in 2 Samuel 7. Nathan approved of David's wish to build the Temple for the ark of the covenant. However, that night God came to Nathan in a dream. God told Nathan that the throne of David's kingdom would be forever. This established that building the kingdom of Israel came before the building of a permanent temple.

Nathan was the one who went to David and made him see his sin in his actions with Bathsheba and Uriah. Because of Nathan David repented (2 Samuel 12).

Nathan and Bathsheba worked together to have David declare Solomon king (1Kings 1:11-37).

Activity: Wise Choices

This activity is meant for ages ten and older. Choose situations by age of participants.

Before the session photocopy and cut apart the "Wise Choice Game Cards" on page 54 and top of page 55.

You may use the "Wise Choice Game Cards" as discussion starters, as roleplays, or as a game. Instructions for each are below.

Discussion Starters: Choose two or more of the cards, depending upon your topic and time.
- Ask a volunteer to read one of the situations.
- Ask participants to vote on which choice is the wisest.
- Let them discuss why they made the choice they did.
- Have them refer back to whatever Scriptures you have been using. Does their choice match up to the Scripture?

Roleplays: Choose two or more of the cards depending upon your topic and time.
- Divide participants into small groups.
- Ask participants to decide how they will present their situation as a roleplay. Their group is to decide which choice they will present as the solution.
- Give each group fifteen to twenty minutes to decide on which choice they will choose, how they will present their roleplay, and time to practice.
- Have each group present their role play. (You may wish to then have the situation and choices read to the whole group and see if the group would have made the wisest choice.)
- After all roleplays have been presented, refer back to whatever Scriptures you have been using. Does their choice match up to the Scripture?

Wise Choices Game: Mix several or all of the cards together and place face down on a table or in a container.
- Have each participant make five "voting cards" by taking four pieces of paper and writing as big as possible "A" on one, "B" on another, "C" on a third, "D" on the fourth, and "E" on the fifth.
- Read or have a volunteer read each situation. Have participants make a choice and hold up their answer, "A," "B," "C," "D," or "E."
- Ask participants to quickly find others who voted as they did and move into that group.
- Move on to the next situation with everyone voting and then quickly finding those who voted as they did. Groups will probably change a little with each vote.
- After all situations have been voted on, refer back to whatever Scriptures you have been using. Do their choices match up to the Scripture(s)?

SOLOMON *(meaning **peaceful**) The third king of Israel. He was able to actually rule as a king instead of being a charismatic warrior leader like Saul and then David.*

*At Solomon's birth Nathan named him **Jedidiah** (meaning **beloved of Yahweh**). But David named him **Solomon** (2 Samuel 12:24-25).*

Solomon is best known for his wisdom, his great wealth, and his building projects, especially the Temple and his palace.

But Solomon did not always use his gift of wisdom, as he is also known for collecting enormous amounts of taxes and for using forced labor to pay for all of this building.

Solomon is also known for disobeying God in his many foreign marriages. He used these marriages as a way of making political friends and keeping his land peaceful.

Because of the great taxes he put on the people, his kingdom was close to rebellion. When Solomon died, so did a united Israel. After his death fighting broke out and the kingdom divided.

Outline of Solomon's Story

- Solomon is born (2 Samuel 12:24-25).

- The prophet Nathan and Solomon's mother, Bathsheba, join together in the struggle to bring Solomon to the throne (1 Kings 1:1-27).

- David names Solomon as king (1 Kings 1:28-53).

- David gives Solomon detailed instructions on how to rule as king, including "Be strong, be courageous, and keep the charge of the LORD your God, walking in his ways and keeping . . . his commandments . . ." (1 Kings 2:1-9).

- Solomon prays to God for wisdom (1 Kings 3:1-15).

- Two women come to Solomon fighting over a baby. All are amazed at Solomon's wise judgment (1 Kings 3:16-28).

- Solomon builds the Temple in the fourth year of his reign (1 Kings 6; 2 Chronicles 2–4).

- Solomon builds his palace and other buildings (1 Kings 7).

- The Temple is dedicated (1 Kings 8).

- God appears to Solomon a second time and promises that if he will walk with God with integrity of heart and uprightness, and following God's commandments, a successor to the throne will not fail (1 Kings 9:1-9).

- The Queen of Sheba visits Solomon (1 Kings 10).

- Solomon makes marriages and alliances with hundreds of foreign women. When he is old, they turn his heart away from God. Because of this the Lord raises up enemies (1 Kings 11).

- Jeroboam (son of a servant of Solomon) rebels against Solomon (1 Kings 11:26-40).

- Solomon dies after reigning for forty years. He is buried in Jerusalem (1 Kings 11:41-43).

- Rehoboam, Solomon's son, succeeds him as king (1 Kings 11:43).

Activity: Wise Choice Game Cards

A group of boys has been bullying you and your best friend in the hallways at school. You're both tired of it.
A. You stand up to the bullies and fight back.
B. You tell your teacher.
C. You tell your dad.
D. You begin to avoid the hallway.
E. Other
_____
_____

You're sick (and probably contagious).
A. You go to school or work anyway and try to stay away from others.
B. You take to your bed and refuse to go to school or work for days.
C. You go to the doctor and see if you can get an excused absence form.
D. You keep track of your fever and other symptoms, returning to work or school when you are sure you are no longer contagious.
E. Other
_____
_____

Six people (including the driver) need to get home from a school event. The car has only five seatbelts.
A. It's not a big deal. The driver promises to drive carefully.
B. You all get in the car, promising to hold on to the sixth person in case of an accident.
C. You try to find a ride home for the sixth person.
D. Two people wait together while the driver drops off three people and then comes back for the last two.
E. Other
_____
_____

You receive a present you don't like.
A. You say thank you and hide it in the closet.
B. You tell the giver it's the best present you ever got and give it to a local charity.
C. You are honest and tell the giver you don't like it, and ask permission to exchange it.
D. You mumble thank you, roll your eyes, and whisper to someone close by that it's ugly.
E. Other
_____
_____

You have just turned twelve but look young for your age. Your mother tells you to go ahead and order from the child's menu because you don't eat that much.
A. You tell your mother that's dishonest.
B. You suggest that your mother ask if anyone can order a child's portion.
C. You don't say anything and order from the child's menu. Your mom is right.
D. You get embarrassed and make a scene.
E. Other
_____
_____

A good friend tells others a secret about you that you had asked your friend not to tell.
A. You forgive your friend even though your friend isn't sorry.
B. You end the friendship, telling your friend he or she can't be trusted.
C. You don't say anything, but you start looking for a new friend.
D. You keep the friendship but tell your friend he or she will have to earn your trust.
E. Other
_____
_____

You have a mission service project and a soccer game at the same time.
A. You tell your coach you're sorry, but the commitment you made to your church is more important.
B. You tell the church you're sorry, but being part of the team means you have to be there for games.
C. You promise to be there for the mission project but call at the last minute to say your coach insists you can't miss the game.
D. You talk your parents into giving some extra money to the mission service project.
E. Other

_____

_____

Your church choir routinely makes copies of music to use for choir practice and sometimes even services.
A. You don't worry about it because it's in a church, and you don't have lots of money.
B. You protest because the church has not purchased blanket permission to use copyrighted music.
C. You check with the church and find out that the church has a purchased a licensing agreement, and it's okay to photocopy the music.
D. You figure no one will ever know. After all, you're not using it to make money, but for worship.
E. Other

_____

_____

Activity: Movies and Choices

View movies or segments of movies as a group, and then together analyze decisions made by characters and what they seemed to base their choices on. Movies will vary with the age group of participants, but even children's movies teach us a lot about moral choices.

It would be helpful to all to discuss the consequences of decisions made.

Some possible movies:

"Amazing Grace"
"Finding Nemo"
"Ice Age"
"Cars"
"The Lion King"
"The Lion, the Witch, and the Wardrobe"

Any current movie that does NOT glorify stealing, killing, or other types of sinful behavior will be suitable.

Caution: Your church must have an Umbrella License® from the Motion Picture Licensing Corporation to show any portion of a film in any setting other than home use. Check with your church office to see if your church has this license before using this activity. For more information see the Motion Picture Licensing Corporation website at www.mplc.com.

Activity: Gleaning Projects

During the study of the story of Ruth or of Jesus feeding the 5000 is a perfect time for a service project that deals with sharing of the abundance of food that we have. Many Americans battle with eating disorders that people without enough to eat cannot even imagine. Perhaps if we learn to leave some of our food dollars for the hungry, we can enrich both our physical and spiritual lives. Here are some possible places to contact for such gleaning service projects:

Plant a Row for the Hungry

Founded by the Garden Writers Association, it encourages gardeners to plant more than they can eat themselves and donate the extra food to a local soup kitchen or food bank.
www.gardenwriters.org/PAR

Church World Service

A mission service organization made up of 35 Protestant, Orthodox, and Anglican denominations in the U.S.

It responds to disasters and works with indigenous organizations to meet human need and help people become self-reliant.
www.churchworldservice.org

Second Harvest Food Bank

Collects canned foods from groups and individuals to distribute to the hungry.

Groups with children can enjoy sorting their donations at their local Second Harvest facility.

Go to their website and click on "Food Bank Locater."
www.secondharvest.org

Catholic Charities USA

A service organization that combines the power of Catholics around the country to reduce poverty and empower communities.
www.catholiccharitiesusa.org

Local Church

Support local church ministries such as:
• Pastor's Discretionary Fund
• Mission Projects
• Church Food Bank
• Providing Food for church families in time of need or grief

Heifer International

Provides animals for starter herds so that families around the world can feed their families on a sustained basis.
www.heifer.org

United Methodist Committee on Relief

Committed to alleviating human suffering no matter what the cause. It responds to disasters and human needs around the world as well as helping people become self-reliant. Overhead is provided by special church collections. All donations to relief go 100% to the relief effort.
www.gbgm-umc.org/umcor

RUTH *(may mean* **companion***) A widow. Daughter-in-law of Naomi. Then wife of Boaz. Mother of Obed. Ancestor of David and Jesus. The Book of Ruth in the Old Testament is named after her and tells her story.*

Ruth was a Moabite. Her husband and his family were Israelites but lived in Moab due to a famine. Her father-in-law, her husband, and her brother-in-law died. She could have returned to her family. But Ruth was devoted to her mother-in-law and returned with her to Bethlehem. Ruth made a choice to be faithful to Naomi's God and to her faith.

So that they would not starve, Naomi was allowed to glean grain from the fields of Boaz. Eventually she married Boaz, and together they had a child named Obed, an ancestor of David.

NAOMI *(meaning either* **my delight** *or* **pleasant***) Wife of Elimelech, mother of Mahlon and Chilion, mother-in-law of Orpah and Ruth. A Hebrew living in the land of Moab.*

Her husband and both sons died. She released her daughters-in-law to go back to their families, but Ruth refused to leave her.

Naomi encouraged Ruth to do her gleaning only in the fields of Boaz.

BOAZ *Husband of Ruth. Relative of Naomi and Elimelech. Father of Obed. Ancestor of David and Jesus.*

Boaz was a wealthy landowner near Bethlehem. He became Ruth's protector, allowing her to glean in his fields.

He married Ruth and became the father of Obed.

Game: Who Am I? Game

Choose the people you are studying or would like to review from the "Who Am I?" game cards on pages 60, 62, 64, 68, 70, 72, 74, 76, 78, 80, and 86. Photocopy the cards and cut them apart. If you have a large number of people, make multiple sets of cards. There should be no more than two teams working on a set of cards at a time to maintain interest.

This game may be played as individuals if you have a small group.

The object of the game is to get the highest score by naming the most people using the fewest number of clues.

DIRECTIONS FOR PLAYING IN GROUPS:

• Mix up cards and place them in a pile face down on a table.

• The first player from the first team gives one clue at a time, in order given on card. After each clue his or her team has a chance to guess the person. IT MUST BE A TEAM GUESS OR POINTS ARE DEDUCTED. You may wish to set a time limit for answering.

• If the first team cannot guess the person after five clues, then the name is read aloud and the card is put in a discard pile. (Depending upon time, you may wish to go through the discard pile when the main pile is completed.)

• The second team's player draws a card and repeats the process with his or her team.

When the cards are all used or you are running out of time (each team must get an equal number of chances), add up the scores.

SCORING:

• Guessing correctly on first clue ....50 points
• Guessing correctly on second clue ....25 points
• Guessing correctly on third clue......................20 points
• Guessing correctly on fourth clue....................15 points
• Guessing correctly on fifth clue ....10 points

• For individual blurting out answer
    and not consulting team ....minus 20 points
• For opposing team blurting out answer...........minus 20 points for opposing team

Teaching through the process of playing a game as a team is a great way for people of all ages to learn teamwork.

EZRA *A priest, a scholar, and an expert in the teachings of Moses. The story of Ezra and Nehemiah is the story of the return of the Jews from exile.*

According to the Bible (starting with Ezra 7), Ezra was sent by King Artaxerxes to Israel to reeducate the Jews in their own faith. Many of the families that had been in exile in Babylonia returned with Ezra to Israel.

NEHEMIAH *A Jew who was a cupbearer to King Artaxerxes in Babylon.*

Nehemiah received news that things were very bad in Jerusalem. He obtained permission from Artaxerxes to return to Jerusalem, where he was appointed governor.

Nehemiah was known for his organizational abilities, and under his supervision the walls of Jerusalem were rebuilt in fifty-two days. It was not an easy task, however, as many of the kingdoms surrounding Jerusalem did not want this to happen. They devised many plots to stop the building, including assassination attempts and false prophecy. But every time Nehemiah understood what was happening, and he dealt with the problem (Nehemiah 6).

Nehemiah also dealt with the injustice he saw in the land. People were forced to mortgage their land and were even forced into slavery to pay their taxes and other debts. Nehemiah canceled all debts. Nehemiah even refused to take his salary as governor (Nehemiah 5).

Nehemiah was governor for twelve years and then returned to Persia. When he returned to Jerusalem years later, his reforms had been neglected and he had to reinstate them.

The Bible does not tell us what happened to either Ezra or Nehemiah, nor does it tell us if their reforms were long lasting.

ADAM
- My name means "earth" or "earthy."
- I am the father of three sons.
- I got in trouble because I gave in to temptation.
- I was given dominion over the animals.
- I am the first man.

NOAH
- I am a righteous man.
- I was thought by my neighbors to be rather strange.
- I was good at building things to specific instructions.
- I had to take care of all kinds of animals for a long time.
- It rained a lot soon after I finished building my ark.

EVE
- I am the mother of three sons.
- I got in trouble because I gave in to temptation.
- My name means "mother of all living."
- I had a conversation with a serpent.
- My husband and I were thrown out of the garden of Eden.

ABRAHAM
- My name was changed when God made a covenant with me.
- I have a nephew named Lot.
- I am the first patriarch of three major religions.
- My son's name is Isaac.
- My name means "father of a multitude."

CAIN
- I am a tiller of the ground by trade.
- I have famous parents.
- I have been condemned to be a wanderer.
- My offering to God was rejected.
- I killed my brother in anger.

SARAH
- My name means "princess."
- I had my first child when I was about 90 years old.
- My name was changed when God made a covenant with my husband and me.
- My son's name is Isaac.
- My husband's name is Abraham.

ABEL
- I am a shepherd.
- I am known for making an acceptable offering to God.
- I have famous parents.
- I am most famous for how I died.
- I was murdered by my brother.

ISAAC
- My name means "he laughs."
- I was born when my parents were very old.
- I am married to Rebekah.
- I was almost sacrificed by my father, but God sent a ram to take my place.
- I have twin sons named Jacob and Esau.

SETH
- I had two brothers.
- Very little is known about me.
- I lived to be 912 years old.
- I am an ancestor of Noah.
- I am the third son of Adam and Eve.

REBEKAH
- I was childless for twenty years after I was married.
- I am the sister of Laban.
- I am the mother of twins.
- People sometimes think I am a schemer, but I am just concerned about my younger son.
- I helped my son Jacob trick his father.

Bible People of Faith

ESTHER

A Jew. An orphan. Cousin of Mordecai. Second wife of Ahasuerus, King of Persia. The Book of Esther is named after her. Her name is probably Persian.

She is known for risking her own life to save the Jews in exile in Persia.

No one seems to know if Esther was a historical person or if her story is a morality tale meant to show the triumph of good over evil and to sustain the Jews in times of great trouble.

The Book of Esther gives the explanation for the Jewish festival of Purim. The word "Purim" means "lots" (as in casting of lots), and the casting of lots plays a large role in the story.

Esther is considered a heroine of the Jewish faith for her selfless courage. Her story is read in its entirety every year at the festival of Purim.

MOREDECAI

Cousin of Esther. He raised the orphaned Esther. A Jew who was an official in the court of King Ahasuerus. He refused to bow to Haman, and therefore Haman decided to slaughter the Jews. Mordecai begged his niece, Esther, to save the Jewish people from extinction.

Outline of Esther's Story

- Vashti, the first wife of King Ahasuerus, is banished for refusing to appear at his banquet (Esther 1).

- Esther hid her relationship to Mordecai and the fact that she was a Jew when she was called along with all the other young women of the kingdom before King Ahasuerus. She was chosen from all the young women to be the second wife of Ahasuerus (Esther 2:1-18).

- Mordecai discovers a plot against the king and tells Esther (Esther 2:19-23).

- Mordecai refuses to bow to Haman, who is a favorite of the king. An angry Haman plans to destroy the Jews on a date determined by the casting of lots (Esther 3).

- Mordecai persuades Esther to go to the king and plead for the Jews (Esther 4).

- Esther invites the king and Haman to a banquet while Haman plots to have Mordecai hanged (Esther 5).

- When the king discovers that it was Mordecai who uncovered the earlier plot against the king, he insists that Haman publicly honor Mordecai (Esther 6).

- At a second banquet with the king and Haman, Esther reveals to the king Haman's plan to have the Jews massacred. The king is angered and orders Haman hanged on the gallows Haman had prepared for Mordecai (Esther 7).

- Since the king's first edict against the Jews cannot be revoked, the king gives Esther and Mordecai his seal and allows them to issue a second edict allowing the Jews to defend themselves (Esther 8).

- The Jews strike down all their enemies with the sword (Esther 9:1-17).

- The festival of Purim is declared (Esther 9:18-32).

- Mordecai's power and fame spread (Esther 10).

JACOB
- I am often thought of as a trickster.
- I made some really good stew.
- I am a twin.
- My name was changed to "Israel" after I wrestled with God.
- I am the father of the twelve tribes of Israel.

MOSES
- I am known as the founder of the Jewish faith.
- I was raised by Egyptians.
- I have a brother and sister who helped me a lot.
- I gave Israel her moral law code.
- I led the Israelites out of Egypt.

ESAU
- I am a hunter.
- I am the firstborn in my family.
- I am a twin.
- I gave up my birthright for a bowl of stew.
- I am Jacob's brother.

MIRIAM
- I am a prophet.
- I had to babysit my little brother.
- I developed a skin disease that was cured through my brother's prayers.
- I led the Israelites in singing after our deliverance from the Red Sea.
- My brothers' names are Aaron and Moses.

RACHEL
- My name means "ewe."
- I am beautiful.
- My husband worked fourteen years in order to marry me.
- I am Jacob's favorite wife.
- I am the mother of Joseph and Benjamin.

AARON
- I was the first priest of Israel.
- I am the ancestor of the Levites, the line of Israel's priests.
- I regret helping the people of Israel make a golden idol out of their jewelry.
- It was my staff that was thrown down in front of Pharaoh. The staff turned into a snake.
- I went with my brother, Moses, to Egypt.

LEAH
- My name means "cow."
- I am the elder daughter of Laban.
- I am Jacob's first wife.
- I am the mother of Jacob's only daughter, Dinah.
- I am the mother of six of the tribes of Israel.

JOSHUA
- My name means "Yahweh is salvation."
- I led the defeat of Israel's enemy, Amalek, while we were wandering with Moses in the wilderness.
- I was an assistant to Moses.
- I was sent as a spy into the land of Canaan and brought back a favorable report.
- After the death of Moses, I became the leader of the Israelites and led them into the Promised Land. I am known for the famous battle of Jericho.

JOSEPH
- I am my father's favorite son.
- My father gave me a coat with long sleeves, and that made my brothers angry.
- I am good at interpreting dreams.
- I helped save Egypt from starvation during a long famine.
- I had my family move to Egypt to join me. That is how centuries later the Israelites became slaves in Egypt.

RAHAB
- I am a resident of Jericho.
- I work as a prostitute so that my family may eat.
- I hid two Israelite spies from the king of Jericho.
- I helped two Israelite spies escape by lowering them down a rope to the other side of the walls of Jericho.
- Because I believed in God and helped the Israelite spies, my family was spared when Jericho fell.

Bible People of Faith

JOB *A very rich man who lived in the land of Uz. He was blameless and upright. He had seven sons and three daughters. He was rich, well known, and probably had a very high social status. He was faithful to God (Job 1:1-5).*

Job's story is about the question, "Why do good people suffer?" While no real reason is given, we learn several things from Job. One is that people's wealth and good health are not always an indication of whether or not a person lives righteously. In Job's day wealth and health were considered a sign of God's favor. Another thing is that all human emotions can be taken to God. Job was angry and told God so, but in the end Job discovered that we cannot possibly know God's will fully.

In the end Job accepted his suffering and remained faithful to God. All of his wealth was restored, and he had ten more children (Job 42:10-13). His neighbors were baffled by this because they figured Job suffered because he had sinned. And if he had sinned, how could everything be restored? There are no easy answers in the Book of Job.

Outline of Job's Story

- Job is a good and righteous man. He is prosperous and faithful to God. Satan challenges Job's character, saying to God that Job is faithful only because nothing bad has happened to him. If bad things happened to Job, he would not be as faithful. God gives permission for Satan to put Job to the test (Job 1:1-12).

- Job loses his property and his children. Job remains faithful (Job 1:13-22).

- Job's entire body is covered with sores. His wife tells him to curse God and die. Job remains faithful to God (Job 2:1-10).

- Job's three friends come to sit with him (Job 2:11-13).

- Job curses the day he was born. From here on Job's speeches are filled with hurt and anger towards God (Job 3).

- Job's friends take turns telling Job that he must have sinned and offended God to have this much misfortune. Job continues to defend himself and God. Job also complains that his suffering is without end (Job 4–28).

- Job defends himself and he complains bitterly (Job 26–27; 29–31).

- Elihu, a younger man who has been sitting quietly, first rebukes Job's friends and then proceeds to rebuke Job for his self-righteousness. He is quite long-winded about it (Job 32–37).

- God answers Job, appearing out of a whirlwind. God asks Job who he is to speak without knowledge, asking Job where he was when God was creating the world and all that is in it (Job 38:1–40:2).

- Job answers God, saying he will respond no further (Job 40:3-5).

- God challenges Job again (Job 40:6–41:34).

- Job repents of his doubts and questioning of God, and once more becomes the faithful Job he had always been (Job 42:1-6).

- Job's friends are reprimanded by God for their speaking wrongly of God (Job 42:7-9).

- Job's fortunes are restowed twofold. Job in his later years has seven sons and three daughters. He lives one-hundred forty years more and sees his children and his children's children, four generations (Job 42:10-17).

DEBORAH
- My name means "bee."
- I am famous for a song I sang in battle.
- I am a woman.
- I rode into battle with Barak.
- I am a prophetess and a judge of Israel.

DAVID
- I am a shepherd.
- I am the youngest son.
- I am good at playing the harp.
- I killed the giant, Goliath, with a stone from my slingshot.
- I am known as the great king of Israel.

GIDEON
- I asked God to give me a sign.
- I am sometimes known as "Jerubbaal" because I pulled down Baal's altar.
- I am often pictured blowing a horn.
- I received a sign from God in the form of a fleece that was very wet even though the ground was dry.
- I was the fifth judge of Israel.

JONATHAN
- My name means "Yahweh has given."
- My father was a king.
- I am known as a great warrior.
- My son's name is Mephibosheth.
- I am a great friend to David.

SAMSON
- I am a nazirite because my mother dedicated me as one.
- I am famous for my long hair.
- I am a judge.
- Delilah cut off my hair, and I lost my great strength.
- I died along with about 3000 Philistines when I pushed down two pillars supporting a house.

MEPHIBOSHETH
- I was five years old when my father died in battle.
- My nurse dropped me.
- I am lame.
- I am Jonathan's son.
- David took me into his household after the death of my father.

SAMUEL
- I am the son of Elkanah and Hannah.
- I was raised by the priest Eli.
- I am a prophet and the last great judge of Israel.
- I anointed Saul as king of Israel.
- I anointed David as the second king of Israel.

ABSALOM
- I am the third son of King David.
- I arranged to have my brother Amnon killed.
- I wanted to succeed my father as king of Israel.
- I rebelled against my father and tried to take the throne.
- I was killed during the rebellion and my death broke my father, David's, heart.

SAUL
- I am from the tribe of Benjamin.
- My name means "asked (of God)."
- I have serious bouts of depression.
- I both hated and loved David.
- I am the first king of Israel.

ABIGAIL
- My name means "my father is joy."
- I was taken captive by the Amalekites.
- My first husband was Nabal, a fool.
- I managed to make peace between David and Nabal.
- When my husband Nabal died, I married David. I went with David to Hebron when he was made king.

Bible People of Faith

Old Testament Prophets

Old Testament Miracles

The list of Old Testament miracles below is not a comprehensive list, but rather a list of some miracles (and where to find them) that would be appropriate for use with children.

Abraham and Sarah
- Birth of Isaac in their old age (Genesis 21)
- Ram being sent to replace Isaac (Genesis 22:13)

Jacob
- God appears to Jacob in a dream (Jacob's ladder) (Genesis 28:10-22)
- Jacob wrestles with God in the form of a man (Genesis 32:22-32)

Moses
- God speaks to Moses from a bush that burns but is not consumed by the fire (Exodus 3)
- The Red Sea parts to let the Israelites cross and leave Egypt (Exodus 14)
- During the Exodus, in the desert, bitter water is made sweet (Exodus 15:22-27)
- Manna is sent from heaven to feed the Israelites (Exodus 16)
- In the wilderness Moses strikes a rock to bring forth water (Exodus 17:1-7)

Daniel and Friends
- God reveals the meaning of Nebuchadnezzar's dreams to Daniel (Daniel 2:17-23)
- Shadrach, Meshach, and Abednego saved from the fiery furnace (Daniel 3)
- A hand writes on the wall at King Belshazzar's feast; Daniel interprets the meaning (Daniel 5)
- Daniel emerges unhurt from the lions' den (Daniel 6)

Elijah
- Ravens sent with food to Elijah (1 Kings 17:1-7)
- Widow's food is multiplied (1 Kings 17:8-16)
- Elijah revives the widow's son (1Kings 17:17-24)
- Fire consumes altar and sacrifice of the prophets of Baal (1 Kings 18:20-40)
- Jordan River is parted (2 Kings 2:6-8)
- A chariot of fire separates Elijah and Elisha; Elijah ascends to heaven in a whirlwind (2 Kings 2:1-12)

Elisha
- Jordan River is parted (2 Kings 2:13-14)
- Spring purified at Jericho (2 Kings 2:19-22)
- Widow's oil is multiplied (2 Kings 4:1-7)
- Boy raised from dead (2 Kings 4:8-37)
- Poison in stew is purified (2 Kings 4:38-41)
- Elisha's food is multiplied to feed one hundred people (2 Kings 4:42-44)
- Naaman healed of leprosy (2 Kings 5:1-14)
- Man brought back to life by touching Elisha's bones (2 Kings 13:20-21)

ISAIAH *(meaning* **Yahweh is salvation***). Son of Amoz. Lived in Jerusalem. One of the greatest prophets of Israel. Isaiah lived from approximately 740 to 700 B.C.*

A prophet to both King Ahaz and King Hezekiah of Judah, the Southern Kingdom. Many think he was either rich and/or from a royal line, but we do not really know for sure. He had a group of disciples, and this may account for part of the book called Second Isaiah (Isaiah 40–55). Some say there is a "Third Isaiah" because these chapters were written about 150 years later than chapters 1-39. This third set of writings is sometimes called "Third Isaiah" from chapters 56 to 66.

All of the Book of Isaiah has the same message. There is criticism of the arrogance and hypocrisy of the leaders in Jerusalem. Isaiah advises kings regarding what will happen to Judah, but they ignore his message. Isaiah also spends a lot of time speaking of injustice.

It is Isaiah who emphasized that a Messiah to lead Israel righteously would come from the line of David, the great king. It is the Book of Isaiah that is most often quoted by Christians when they identify Jesus the Messiah. Many of our richest images of the Messiah come from Isaiah.

Some Words from Isaiah

- He shall judge between the nations, and shall arbitrate for many peoples; they shall beat their swords into plowshares, and their spears into pruning hooks; nation shall not lift up sword against nation, neither shall they learn war any more (Isaiah 2:4).

- For a child has been born for us, a son given to us . . . (Isaiah 9:6-7).

- A shoot shall come out from the stump of Jesse, and a branch shall grow out of his roots . . . (known as the "peaceful kingdom") (Isaiah 11:1-9).

- A voice cries out: "In the wilderness prepare the way of the LORD, make straight in the desert a highway for our God . . . " (Isaiah 40:3-5).

- Here is my servant, whom I uphold, my chosen, in whom my soul delights; I have put my spirit upon him; he will bring forth justice to the nations. . . . (Isaiah 42:1-4).

- . . . He was wounded for our transgressions, crushed for our iniquities; upon him was the punishment that made us whole, and by his bruises we are healed (known as the "suffering servant" (Isaiah 52:13–53:12).

- The spirit of the Lord GOD is upon me, because the LORD has anointed me; he has sent me to bring good news to the oppressed, to bind up the brokenhearted, to proclaim liberty to the captives, and release to the prisoners . . . (Isaiah 61:1-4).

BATHSHEBA
- My name means "daughter of abundance."
- I was married to Uriah.
- I committed adultery with King David.
- I married King David after my husband Uriah died.
- I am the mother of King Solomon.

BOAZ
- I am a wealthy landowner near Bethlehem.
- I am an ancestor of David and Jesus.
- I allowed Ruth to glean grain from my fields.
- I am married to Ruth.
- I am the father of Obed.

NATHAN
- I am a prophet.
- God came to me in a dream to tell me that David would not build the Temple, but that his kingdom would be established forever.
- I helped both David and his son Solomon.
- I made David understand his sins and his need to repent.
- I worked with Bathsheba to make Solomon king of Israel.

EZRA
- I am a priest.
- I know a lot about the teachings of Moses.
- I lived during the time the Jews began to return from exile.
- I was sent back to Jerusalem from the Exile in Babylonia.
- I helped Jews relearn the Jewish faith.

SOLOMON
- I am a king of Israel.
- I married many foreign wives.
- I was very wealthy and taxed my people heavily for building projects.
- I built the Temple.
- I am famous for my great wisdom.

NEHEMIAH
- I was a cupbearer for King Artaxerxes in Babylon.
- I was appointed governor of Jerusalem.
- I supervised the rebuilding of the walls of Jerusalem. It took only 52 days.
- I refused to take a salary as governor.
- I went to Persia. When I returned years later, my reforms had been forgotten and I had to start again.

RUTH
- I am an ancestor of David and Jesus.
- I am a Moabite.
- I am the mother of Obed.
- I followed my mother-in-law, Naomi, and I came to worship her God.
- I married Boaz.

ESTHER
- I am very beautiful.
- I am an orphan.
- I became queen when I became the second wife of King Ahasuerus of Persia.
- I have a cousin named Mordecai.
- There is a book of the Bible which bears my name.

NAOMI
- I am a Hebrew who lived in the land of Moab.
- My name means "my delight" or "pleasant."
- My husband and both sons died and left me with two daughters-in-law to care for.
- I am the mother-in-law of Ruth.
- I encourage Ruth to do her gleaning only in the fields of Boaz.

MORDECAI
- I am a Jew, but am an official in the court of King Ahasuerus.
- I raised my orphaned cousin.
- I refused to bow down to Haman, the prime minister.
- Haman plotted to have me hanged and the Jews slaughtered.
- I convinced Esther to go to the king and save the Jews, and I became powerful and famous.

Bible People of Faith

JEREMIAH *(a prophet from 626 to 587 B.C.)* Prophet to the Southern

Kingdom of Judah. He was called to be a prophet in the thirteenth year of the reign of King Josiah (Jeremiah 1:1-2). He was a young man, maybe in his early twenties, when he was called, although he had been consecrated while in his mother's womb (Jeremiah 1:5). He was a prophet for forty years and to five kings: Josiah, Jehoahaz, Jehoiakim, Jehoiachin, and Zedekiah.

Jeremiah supported the reforms of Josiah (621 B.C.). But most of his prophetic life was spent calling Judah to repentance and predicting the downfall of the nation because of their abandonment of God in favor of foreign gods. Jeremiah's condemnations of the Jews of the time did not make him very popular.

Jeremiah was quite a character. There are many symbolic lessons he tried to bring to the people, such as potter's clay (Jeremiah 18:1-11) and the yoke he wore to demonstrate that the people were going to be forced to submit to the yoke of Babylon's control (Jeremiah 27).

While predicting Judah's downfall, Jeremiah also demonstrated hope in the people's eventual return to the land by buying a field in his homeland. He also declared the establishment of a new covenant with God.

Knowing his age at the time and the long duration of the Exile, it is probable that Jeremiah died in exile from his beloved homeland.

Some Words from Jeremiah

- Obey my voice, and I will be your God, and you shall be my people; and walk only in the way that I command you, so that it may be well with you (Jeremiah 7:23).

- The days are surely coming, says the LORD, when I will raise up for David a righteous Branch, and he shall reign as king and deal wisely, and shall execute justice and righteousness in the land (Jeremiah 23:5).

- I will give them a heart to know that I am the LORD; and they shall be my people and I will be their God, for they shall return to me with their whole heart (Jeremiah 24:7).

- Now therefore amend your ways and your doings, and obey the voice of the LORD your God, and the LORD will change his mind about the disaster that he has pronounced against you (Jeremiah 26:13).

- Then when you call upon me and come and pray to me, I will hear you. When you search for me, you will find me; if you seek me with all your heart, I will let you find me . . . (Jeremiah 29:12-14).

- The days are surely coming, says the LORD, when I will make a new covenant with the house of Israel and the house of Judah (Jeremiah 31:31).

JOB
- I am a good and righteous man, faithful to God.
- I lost my wife, children, health, and wealth.
- I had some friends who weren't really very comforting in my troubles; they blamed me.
- My fortune was restored, and I had more sons and daughters.
- I am known for my patience.

JOSIAH
- I became king of Judah at the age of eight.
- I am known as a reformer king.
- I decided to rebuild the Temple.
- During the rebuilding of the Temple the Book of Deuteronomy was found.
- I brought the people back to the worship and laws of Yahweh.

ISAIAH
- I am a prophet.
- My name means "Yahweh is Salvation."
- I am known as one of the greatest prophets of Israel.
- I criticized the kings of Israel for their arrogance and hypocrisy.
- I wrote many words about the coming Messiah, and a lot of those words are read in Christian churches at Christmas.

HULDAH
- My name means "weasel."
- My husband was keeper of the wardrobe.
- I am a prophetess.
- I was consulted by King Josiah about the Book of Deuteronomy he found.
- I predicted the downfall of Judah, but said it would not be until after the death of Josiah because of his faithfulness to God.

JEREMIAH
- I am a prophet.
- I was consecrated by God before I was born.
- I used symbols such as potter's clay and the yoke of an ox to show people what I meant.
- I predicted Judah's downfall, but was also hopeful and bought a field in my homeland just before I was taken off to exile.
- I said that the Lord would raise up a just and righteous king from the righteous Branch of David.

DANIEL
- I am a prophet.
- I was taken to Babylon as part of the Exile.
- I was a court official, but known for keeping the dietary laws of the Jewish faith.
- The book of the Bible with my name on it is an apocalyptic book.
- I was thrown to the lions but survived.

ELIJAH
- I am a prophet.
- My name means "Yahweh is my God."
- I was taken to heaven in a chariot in a whirlwind.
- A place is set for me at the Passover table each year.
- At the Transfiguration I was seen talking with Jesus and Moses.

SHADRACH, MESHACH, and ABEDNEGO
- We were taken to Babylon as part of the Exile.
- We are friends of Daniel's.
- God gave us knowledge and skill in literature and wisdom.
- We refused to worship a golden statue of the king.
- We were thrown into a fiery furnace and survived.

ELISHA
- I am a prophet.
- I am bald.
- My name means "God is salvation."
- My message is that God condemns sin, but shows mercy and love to the faithful. God cares for the everyday needs of people.
- I was personally trained by Elijah.

HOSEA
- I am a prophet.
- My name may mean "salvation."
- My marriage was a symbol of God's relationship to Israel.
- I am from the Northern Kingdom.
- My message is that God forgives those who truly repent and ask for forgiveness.

Bible People of Faith

ELIJAH (meaning **Yahweh is my God**)

Prophet of Israel during the reigns of Ahab, Ahaziah, and Jehoram (869-842 B.C.). Elijah's story is a struggle for the survival of the faith of Yahweh in the tradition of Moses. Israel had become corrupted with the worship of Baal and other foreign gods. At that time there were also other "prophets" of Yahweh who disagreed on issues of faith. For Elijah the issue was following the laws of Moses.

See page 66 for a list of some of the miracle stories associated with Elijah.

Elijah's story is recorded in First and Second Kings, but he is also spoken of in 2 Chronicles 21:12-15, Ezra 10:21, and Malachi 4:5. His name is to be found in the New Testament in relationship to Jesus.

Tradition associates Elijah with the prophet that shall come to prepare Israel for the day of Judgment. Even today at Passover a place is set for Elijah. In the New Testament some thought Jesus might be Elijah returned (Mark 8:28). And it was with Moses and Elijah that Jesus was seen at the Transfiguration (Matthew 17:3).

We know nothing of Elijah's birth, but we do know of the end of his time on earth. Elijah is said not to have died, but to have been taken up to heaven in a chariot of fire in a whirlwind (2 Kings 2:1-11).

Elijah's message: We are to put God first in our lives and follow God's laws.

ELISHA (meaning **God is salvation**).

A prophet from the Northern Kingdom of Israel. Successor to Elijah, who personally trained Elisha. He was a prophet during the time of kings Jehoram, Jehu, Jehoahaz, and Jehoash (842-786 B.C.). There are many miracle stories concerning Elisha (see page 66).

Elisha's story begins in 1 Kings 19:19. Like other prophets Elisha advised kings. Since he was from the Northern Kingdom of Israel, he advised the kings of the north. Elisha also spent much time alleviating the needs of the poor. His story continues through 2 Kings 13:21, which tells of Elisha's death and yet another miracle of a man brought back to life when he was thrown into Elisha's grave. Upon touching Elisha's bones, the man immediately came to life.

The only mention of Elisha in the New Testament is in Luke 4:27.

Elisha did have somewhat of a temper. Second Kings 2:23-24 tells of a group of small boys that made fun of his baldness, and he cursed them. Forty-two of them were mauled by bears.

Elisha's message: God condemns sin. God shows mercy and love to the faithful. God cares for the everyday needs of people.

JOEL

- I am a prophet.
- My name means "Yahweh is God."
- My book in the Bible describes a great plague of locusts.
- I say disaster comes when the people turn from God.
- My message is that salvation can only come by turning back to God.

NAHUM

- I am a prophet.
- I am from southern Judah.
- My book interprets the fall of Nineveh.
- I teach that those who do evil and oppress others will be punished.
- My message is that God "is slow to anger but great in power, and the Lord will by no means clear the guilty."

AMOS

- I am a prophet.
- I am from Teokoa in the Southern Kingdom but am a prophet to the Northern Kingdom.
- I live in prosperous times in Israel.
- I criticize the people of Israel for living unrighteously.
- I am famous for having said, "Let justice roll down like waters."

HABAKKUK

- I am a prophet.
- People know almost nothing about me.
- I was upset about all the cruelty of the leaders.
- I withdrew to a watchtower and waited for God to answer my questions.
- God answered me that people would be punished when God decides the time is right.
- My message is that God is my strength.

OBADIAH

- I am a prophet.
- My name means "Servant of Yahweh."
- My book is the shortest one in the Old Testament.
- I predicted that one day Judah would be restored.
- My message is that God rules.

ZEPHANIAH

- I am a prophet.
- My name means "Yahweh protects" or "Yahweh has hidden."
- I prophesied during the time of young King Josiah.
- I denounced corruption, injustice, and the worship of foreign gods and warned that all nations will be judged for their evil ways, but after judgment God's mercy will be offered to all.
- My message is that the day of the Lord is near.

JONAH

- I am a prophet.
- My name means "dove."
- I am often called the reluctant prophet.
- I was called by God to preach repentance to Nineveh.
- I was swallowed and then spit out by a large fish.

HAGGAI

- I am a prophet.
- My name means "born on a festival."
- I tried to get the people to begin working on the Temple once again.
- I told the people the Temple was the symbol of where their hearts are.
- My message is that the Lord will bless you.

MICAH

- I am a prophet.
- My name means "Who is like Yahweh?"
- I warned the people to return to the law of God and to pure worship.
- I said that everyone must live justly.
- My message is that God has told you "what is good; and what does the LORD require of you but to do justice, and to love kindness, and to walk humbly with your God?"

ZECHARIAH

- I am a prophet.
- My name means "Yahweh remembers."
- I had eight visions.
- I called people to live faithfully and with justice.
- I said many things that are quoted in the New Testament to describe the Messiah.

JOSIAH *King of Judah from 640 to 609* B.C. *Josiah was only eight years old when he became king. He was a reformer king.*

Josiah's father, Amon, was as corrupt as the kings before him and abandoned the worship of Yahweh. He was killed by his servants, and Josiah became king.

Josiah is known as the faithful king. "He did what was right in the sight of the LORD" (2 Kings 22:2). In the eighteenth year of his reign, he decided to rebuild the Temple. During the renovation of the Temple, Hilkiah, the high priest, discovered the "Book of Law." Tradition says this book was Deuteronomy. Shaphan, his secretary, read the book aloud to Josiah. Huldah was consulted about the book, and because of what she had to say, Josiah immediately instituted reforms. He not only brought Judah back to the worship and laws of Yahweh, but he carried his reforms into Samaria.

In 609 B.C. *Josiah was killed at Megiddo by Pharaoh Neco, who was on his way to join forces with the king of Assyria. Josiah died before the fall of Judah (2 Kings 23:28-30).*

HULDAH *(meaning* **weasel***) A prophetess. Wife of Shallum, the keeper of the wardrobe (probably either the royal wardrobe or the priestly wardrobe).*

Josiah had the scrolls of the "book" that was found brought to Huldah. Huldah predicted the downfall of Judah, but that it would not happen until after the death of Josiah because of his faithfulness (2 Kings 22:14-20).

It is not known for sure why Huldah was consulted instead of Jeremiah. At least three different explanations have been given: 1) Jeremiah was out of town, 2) Huldah was the wife of the keeper of the wardrobe and therefore close at hand, and 3) Josiah thought a woman would deal more gently with him than the very tough Jeremiah.

Jewish tradition says that Huldah and Jeremiah were related in some way.

MALACHI

- I am a prophet.
- My name means "my messenger."
- I denounced sloppy worship practices and the failure to pay tithes.
- I denounced injustice and exploitation.
- My message is that people must repent and live righteously.

ELIZABETH

- I didn't have a child until I was older.
- I am married to a priest.
- I am the wife of Zechariah.
- I am related to Mary, the mother of Jesus.
- I am the mother of John the Baptist.

JESUS

- I am related to Zechariah and Elizabeth.
- I am a descendant of David.
- I went without eating for forty days in the wilderness.
- I was wrongly accused of a crime.
- I am the Alpha and the Omega, the Messiah.

SIMEON

- I am a righteous and devout man in Jerusalem.
- I was promised I would not die before I saw the Messiah.
- I was guided to the Temple by the Holy Spirit on the day Jesus was brought to be dedicated.
- I held the baby Jesus in my arms.
- I prophesied that Mary would suffer because of opposition to her son.

MARY

- I am a very important person.
- I had to flee with my family to Egypt.
- I am related to Elizabeth.
- I had a visit from the angel of the Lord.
- I asked my son to change water into wine at a wedding party.

ANNA

- I am a prophet.
- I never left the temple but worshiped day and night.
- My story is told in Luke 2:36-38.
- I was 84 years old when Jesus was born.
- I was in the temple when Jesus was brought for his dedication, and I praised God.

JOSEPH

- Not very much is known about me.
- An angel visited me in a dream.
- I am a righteous man.
- I had to take my family to Bethlehem to be counted in a census.
- I am a carpenter by trade.

JOHN THE BAPTIST

- I am a prophet.
- I was executed by Herod Antipas.
- I wear clothing made of camel's hair, and locusts and honey is my favorite meal.
- I preach about repenting of our sins.
- I baptized Jesus.

ZECHARIAH

- I am a priest.
- The angel Gabriel appeared to me to tell me I would have a son.
- I was struck dumb because I didn't believe the angel.
- I am married to Elizabeth.
- I am the father of John the Baptist.

PETER

- I used to be a Galilean fisherman.
- I am a disciple.
- I was one of Jesus' inner circle.
- I denied knowing Jesus three times on the night he was arrested.
- Jesus called me "rock" and entrusted me to build his church.

Bible People of Faith

DANIEL *(meaning* **God is my judge***) A young Jewish prophet (597-538 B.C.). Along with others Daniel was taken out of Israel as part of the Babylonian Exile.*

He and his three friends Shadrach, Meshach, and Abednego were considered healthy, handsome, and wise. They were taken into King Nebuchadnezzar's court to be trained. They were given the best of the rich food and drink in the kingdom. However, they refused to abandon Jewish dietary laws. Daniel was a court official under kings Nebuchadnezzar (Nebuchadnessor), Belshazzar, and Darius.

Daniel is known for his faithfulness to God and for his ability to interpret dreams. He is also famous for surviving the lions' den because God sent an angel to protect his faithful servant (Daniel 6).

Daniel is also known for his visions. The Book of Daniel is the only apocalyptic book of the Old Testament (Apocalypse *means* to reveal.)

Daniel has come to stand for the courage to do the right thing even during very difficult circumstances.

Outline of Daniel's Story

• Daniel and friends at the Babylonian court (Daniel 1).

• Nebuchadnezzar has a dream, and the interpretation is revealed to Daniel by God. Daniel and his friends are promoted (Daniel 2).

• Nebuchadnezzar has a second dream. Daniel interprets the dream, predicting the king's expulsion from society until he acknowledges the power of God. The dream comes true, and after his exile Nebuchadnezzar praises God (Daniel 4).

• King Belshazzar has a great feast. A disembodied hand writes a message on the wall and Daniel interprets it (Daniel 5).

• During the reign of Darius, Daniel is thrown into the lions' den but remains unharmed (Daniel 6).

• Daniel has visions of four beasts. He also has visions of a ram and a goat, which are interpreted by Gabriel as a vision of the time of the end (Daniel 7-8).

• Daniel prays for the people (Daniel 9).

• Daniel's final vision is of a conflict between earthly and heavenly power, and a promise of resurrection (Daniel 10-12).

JUDAS ISCARIOT
- I am a disciple.
- I am one of the disciples whose name is easy to remember.
- I was with Jesus when Mary of Bethany poured oil on his feet.
- I am the treasurer of the group.
- I betrayed Jesus.

PHILIP
- I was the first Christian missionary.
- I am a disciple.
- I answered Jesus' question about wages in the story of Jesus feeding the five thousand.
- I introduced Nathanael to Jesus.
- My name is very common, even today.

ANDREW
- I used to be a fisherman.
- I am a disciple.
- My name means "manly."
- I introduced my brother to Jesus.
- It is said I was martyred in Greece and died on an X-shaped cross.

SIMON THE ZEALOT
- I am a disciple.
- I usually have a couple of words attached to my first name.
- Some people think I have radical political views.
- No one knows, but because of my name some people think I have a violent nature.
- I have also been called the "Cananaean."

BARTHOLOMEW
- I am a disciple.
- I wasn't sure about Jesus until he told me things about myself he had no way of knowing.
- My name means "gift of God."
- I am sometimes known as Nathanael.
- I traveled as a missionary to Egypt, Persia, India, and Armenia.

THOMAS
- I am a disciple.
- My name is common, even today.
- My story is told in the Gospel of John.
- My name means "twin."
- I am often called "doubting" because I didn't believe in the Resurrection until I had proof.

JUDAS SON OF JAMES
- Not very much is known about me.
- I am a disciple.
- Another disciple has the same first name and that's why I'm called "son of."
- In the Book of Mark I am called Thaddaeus.
- I traveled a lot as a missionary.

JAMES SON OF ALPHAEUS
- I am a disciple.
- I have the same first name as another disciple.
- I am sometimes known as "the younger" or "little," probably because I was shorter than the other disciple with the same first name.
- I'm always known as "son of."
- Tradition says that I was martyred for my faith.

MATTHEW
- I am a disciple.
- It was Jesus himself who called me to be a disciple.
- My name appears in every list of the disciples.
- I was a tax collector before my call.
- I am the writer of one of the Gospels.

JAMES
- I am a disciple.
- I have the same first name as another disciple.
- I am one of the three disciples closest to Jesus.
- My brother was a disciple too.
- My brother and I used to argue about who would sit on Jesus' right hand in the kingdom of heaven.

SHADRACH

MESHACH

ABEDNEGO

SHADRACH, MESHACH, AND ABEDNEGO

Friends of Daniel. They were taken to Babylon as part of the Exile. They were considered healthy, handsome, and wise. They were taken into King Nebuchadnezzar's court to be trained. They were given the best of the rich food and drink in the kingdom. However, they refused to abandon the strict Jewish dietary laws. Because of their faithfulness (along with Daniel's), God gave them knowledge and skill in every aspect of literature and wisdom (Daniel 1:17).

Their Hebrew names were changed by the palace master: "Hananiah he called Shadrach, Mishael he called Meshach, and Azariah he called Abednego" (Daniel 1:7b).

When King Nebuchadnezzar made a golden statue and issued a decree that all in the land must bow down and worship it, these three young men refused to do so. Because of this they were thrown into a fiery furnace. The raging flames were so strong that they killed the men who actually put the three into the furnace. However, four men were seen walking around in the furnace (the fourth is thought to be an angel of God).

Their survival impressed Nebuchadnezzar so much that he made a new decree that none should say anything bad about the God of these three men. The three were given promotions (Daniel 3).

JOHN
- I am a disciple.
- I have a brother who is also a disciple.
- I am part of Jesus' inner circle.
- I am thought to be the disciple "whom Jesus loved."
- When he died on the cross, Jesus asked me to take care of his mother, and I did.

ZACCHAEUS
- I am from Jericho.
- I am a follower of Jesus.
- I was a tax collector.
- I repented of my sins and made extra repayment to those I had cheated.
- I am best known for being short and climbing a tree.

MARY MAGDALENE
- I am a follower of Jesus.
- Jesus cured me of seven demons.
- I was at the crucifixion of Jesus.
- I was at the tomb and was one of the first to learn of Jesus' resurrection.
- I am always called by both my first and last names.

JOANNA
- I am a follower of Jesus.
- I was cured of an illness by Jesus.
- I helped provide food and money for Jesus and the disciples.
- I was at the Crucifixion.
- I was at the empty tomb on the morning of Jesus' resurrection.

MARTHA
- I am a follower and a friend of Jesus.
- My name means "lady."
- I live in Bethany with my brother and my sister.
- I was one of the first to call Jesus "the Messiah."
- I am always the one responsible for taking care of guests when they visit our home.

NICODEMUS
- I am a Pharisee.
- I am a member of the Sanhedrin.
- I came in the middle of the night to ask Jesus many questions.
- I defended Jesus before the Sanhedrin.
- I provided a hundred pounds of myrrh and aloes for Jesus' burial.

MARY OF BETHANY
- I am a follower and a friend of Jesus.
- I am known for my great devotion to Jesus.
- I anointed Jesus' feet with expensive oil and made Judas angry.
- I live in Bethany with my brother and my sister.
- I sat at Jesus' feet to listen when he visited our home. My sister was upset with me.

JOSEPH OF ARIMATHEA
- I am a secret follower of Jesus.
- I am a member of the Sanhedrin.
- I am a rich man.
- I moved to Jerusalem and had to purchase land.
- I provided the tomb for Jesus' burial.

LAZARUS
- I am a follower and a friend of Jesus.
- Not very much is known about me, though I caused Jesus a lot of trouble (not on purpose).
- I have two sisters who don't always get along.
- I was almost put to death because Jesus performed a miracle for me.
- Jesus raised me from the dead.

SIMON OF CYRENE
- I am a follower of Jesus.
- I have two sons, Alexander and Rufus.
- Not much is known about me.
- My story is told in three of the Gospels.
- I carried the crossbar of Jesus' cross.

Bible People of Faith

HOSEA *(may mean* **salvation***). This is the first book of the minor prophets. Prophet of the Northern Kingdom of Israel (755-725 B.C.).*

Hosea's marriage to Gomer is a symbol of God's relationship to Israel.

Hosea's message: When we sin, we separate ourselves from God. When we sin, we must suffer the consequences of that sin. God gives forgiveness to those who truly repent and ask for forgiveness.

JOEL *(meaning* **Yahweh is God***). A prophet. Time not exactly known.*

The Book of Joel described a great plague of locusts (type of grasshopper). They were very destructive and had eaten all the crops. Then there came a severe drought. Because of this there was a terrible famine in the land. To Joel these disasters came because the people again were turning from God.

Joel's message: Salvation can only come by turning back to God.

AMOS *A prophet (760-745 B.C.). He was from Tekoa (Amos 1:1), a town in the Southern Kingdom, but he was a prophet to the Northern Kingdom.*

The times in which Amos lived were good times for Israel. The people were very prosperous. Amos, however, saw the contrast between how the rich and the poor lived. Amos began by preaching against Israel's neighbors and how they were unjust. Then, just when the Israelites began to pay attention to him, he pronounced God's judgment on Israel. Israel too was living unrighteously and would feel God's punishment. Though he preached of Israel's destruction, he also spoke of the restoration of David's kingdom.

Amos' message: "Let justice roll down like waters, and righteousness like an everflowing stream" (Amos 5:24).

OBADIAH *(meaning* **servant of Yahweh***). A prophet (after 587 B.C.).*

His book is the shortest in the Old Testament, just one chapter of twenty-one verses. The Book of Obadiah said that the Edomites (a long-time enemy of Israel) would be punished by God for their sins. He also said that Judah would be restored.

Obadiah's message: God rules. God will see that Edom is punished for its sins and the land returned to God's people.

CENTURION AT THE CROSS
- I have high social status.
- I am a Roman.
- No one knows my name.
- I was at the Crucifixion.
- I am the commander of a Roman centuria.

JOHN MARK
- I am a Jewish Christian.
- I traveled with Paul and Barnabas.
- Christians prayed at my mother's house when Peter was in prison.
- I'm Barnabas' cousin.
- I wrote one of the Gospels.

STEPHEN
- I am a follower of Jesus.
- I am known for being full of grace.
- I am a Greek-speaking Jew.
- I was chosen by the disciples to help serve the community.
- I am the first Christian martyr.

BARNABAS
- I am from Cyprus.
- I am a very important convert to Christianity.
- My name means "son of encouragement."
- I traveled with Paul.
- Paul and I went our separate ways after an argument over my cousin John Mark.

PAUL
- I am a follower of Jesus.
- I did not know Jesus.
- I traveled to a lot of places as a missionary.
- I wrote letters.
- I was converted when I saw Jesus in a blinding light on the road to Damascus.

TIMOTHY
- I traveled with Paul.
- I am a Gentile convert from Lystra.
- My mother was a Jewish Christian, and my father was Greek.
- I have a very good reputation among the believers in Lystra and Iconium.
- Two letters Paul wrote me are in the New Testament.

ANANIAS
- The Lord came to me in a vision.
- I am a disciple in Damascus.
- I did not like Paul.
- I restored Paul's sight.
- I baptized Paul.

EUNICE
- I am married to a Greek.
- I live in Lystra.
- I am a Jewish Christian.
- I raised my son in the Christian faith.
- I am Timothy's mother.

SILAS
- I am a member of the Jerusalem church.
- I am also known as Silvanus.
- I was chosen by Barnabas and Paul to carry the agreement made at the Jerusalem Conference to the church in Antioch.
- In Philippi I was thrown in jail along with Paul.
- I was with Paul when he wrote some of his letters.

LOIS
- I am mentioned in the Bible only once.
- I am a Christian convert.
- I live in Lystra.
- The Bible commends me for my faith.
- I am Timothy's grandmother.

JONAH *(meaning **dove**) The reluctant prophet. When most children think of Jonah, they think of him as being swallowed by a whale (actually the Bible says "large fish" (Jonah 1:17). Parts of his story are well known to children. The rest of the story is interesting and very visual as well. (See the outline of his story below.)*

The Book of Jonah cannot be dated, although many have tried to do so.

Jonah was the son of Amittai. He was very different from other prophets. We do not have any words of prophecy that he spoke except those words delivered to the king of the Ninevites, calling him to repent.

The Book of Jonah is Jonah's story, that of a man trying to escape from a task he did not want to perform. He was asked to go to Nineveh to proclaim that the city would be destroyed. However, Jonah knew that if he preached to Nineveh the Ninevites would repent, and God would not destroy them. That would ruin his credibility as a prophet. (Not only that but the Ninevites were heartily disliked by Jonah, and he didn't want God to save them.) This was quite a dilemma for a prophet! Jonah's inward struggles and his conflict with God help us look at our own struggles with God's call for our lives.

Outline of Jonah's Story

- God calls Jonah to go to Nineveh (Jonah 1:1-2).

- Jonah tries to get away from God by taking a ship to Tarshish (Jonah 1:3).

- God causes a great storm, and the sailors cast lots to see who has angered a god. The lot falls on Jonah. He requests to be thrown overboard (Jonah 1:4-16).

- God sends a large fish to swallow Jonah. He is in the belly of the fish for three days and three nights (Jonah 1:17).

- Jonah offers a prayer of thanksgiving to God. He agrees to do as God has asked. The fish spews Jonah out onto dry land (Jonah 2).

- Jonah goes to Nineveh and cries out, "Forty days more and Nineveh shall be overthrown!" The people of Nineveh believe God's word as spoken by Jonah (Jonah 3:1-5).

- The king of Nineveh covers himself in sackcloth and sits in ashes (both a sign of repentance and mourning). The king decrees that all humans and animals shall fast and be covered with sackcloth (Jonah 3:6-9).

- God changes his mind and spares Nineveh (Jonah 3:10).

- Jonah gets angry and complains to God. He tells God he would rather die than live (Jonah 4:1-3).

- God questions Jonah's right to be angry (Jonah 4:4).

- Jonah makes a booth to shade himself. God causes a bush to grow over Jonah to give shade. Jonah is very happy. But when dawn comes, God appoints a worm to attack the bush. Jonah again declares he would rather die (Jonah 4:5-8).

- God gives Jonah a lecture. God says that Jonah is concerned about one bush for which he did not labor. God states that God is concerned about a great city with more than one hundred and twenty thousand persons (Jonah 4:9-11).

MICAH *(meaning* **Who is like Yahweh?***) Micah was a prophet from Moresheth in the days of kings Jotham, Ahaz, and Hezekiah of Judah (Micah 1:1). He was a prophet from before 722 to 701 B.C. Micah lived in rural surroundings, but was familiar with the corruption of city life. He saw the fall of the Northern Kingdom of Israel. Because of this he warned the kings of Judah (the Southern Kingdom) to return to the law of God and to pure worship. Micah condemned the wealthy landowners for taking advantage of the poor. He condemned wicked rulers and wicked prophets. He emphasized that all should live with justice. He did have a message of hope for restoration after the Exile (Book of Micah).*

Micah's message: "He has told you, O mortal, what is good; and what does the LORD require of you but to do justice, and to love kindness, and to walk humbly with your God?" (Micah 6:8).

NAHUM *(625-612 B.C.) He was from Elkosh, in southern Judah (Nahum 1:1). The Book of Nahum interprets the fall of Nineveh. Nahum saw Nineveh's fall as a great blessing for Israel. Nahum taught that those who turn away from God and do evil and oppress others will someday be punished.*

Nahum's message: "The LORD is slow to anger but great in power, and the LORD will by no means clear the guilty" (Nahum 1:3).

HABAKKUK *(608-598 B.C.) (meaning* **embrace** *in Hebrew, or* **fruit tree** *in Akkadian) Almost nothing is known about the prophet himself.*

Habakkuk saw himself surrounded with lawlessness and injustice and cried out to God, asking how long this injustice would go on without punishment. When God answered that the current rulers would be defeated, Habakkuk was not comforted because he saw that the cruelty of the Babylonian empire was even worse. He protested to God, wondering how long this cycle would go on with one set of rulers worse than another taking over. He then withdrew to his watchtower to wait for the answer.

God answered that the time was coming when the wicked would be punished, but that punishment would come when God thought the time was right. "For there is still a vision for the appointed time; it speaks of the end, and does not lie. If it seems to tarry, wait for it; it will surely come, it will not delay. Look at the proud! Their spirit is not right in them, but the righteous live by their faith" (Habakkuk 2:3-4).

Habakkuk's message: "GOD, the Lord, is my strength" (Habakkuk 3:19a).

ZEPHANIAH *(meaning* **Yahweh protects** *or* **Yahweh has hidden***)*

(630-620 B.C.). Zephaniah prophesied during the reign of the young King Josiah. He denounced corruption, injustice, and the worship of foreign gods. He warned that all nations would be judged for their evil ways, but after judgment God's mercy would be offered to all.

Zephaniah's message: "The great day of the LORD is near, near and hastening fast" (Zephaniah 1:14a).

HAGGAI *(meaning* **born on a festival***) (520 B.C.) It was eighteen years*

after the people had returned from the Babylonian Exile, and all work had stopped on the Temple in Jerusalem (Ezra 4:24). Haggai tried to rouse the people to begin working on the Temple once again. He told of the importance of the rebuilding of the Temple, because the Temple was (and still is) the symbol of where the hearts of the people were.

Haggai's message: "From this day on I will bless you" (Haggai 2:19c).

ZECHARIAH *(meaning* **Yahweh remembers***) (520-518 B.C.) Zechariah*

was a very popular name. Like the prophet Haggai, Zechariah also urged the people to return to the work of rebuilding the Temple. Zechariah had eight visions (Zechariah 1-6). An angel of the Lord interpreted the visions for Zechariah. These visions told Zechariah that the Temple would be rebuilt. Zechariah called for living faithfully and with justice (Zechariah 7-9). In Zechariah there are many passages used in the New Testament to describe the coming Messiah (Zechariah 9–14).

Zechariah's messianic message: "Lo, your king comes to you; triumphant and victorious is he, humble and riding on a donkey, on a colt, the foal of a donkey" (Zechariah (9:9b).

MALACHI *(meaning* **my messenger***) (500-450 B.C.) Malachi lived in*

Jerusalem just before the return of Ezra and Nehemiah along with the exiles. He denounced the sloppy worship practices of the people, their giving of blemished animals for sacrifice, and their failure to pay tithes. He also denounced injustice and exploitation. He said the people must repent and live righteously.

Malachi's message: "But for you who revere my name the sun of righteousness shall rise, with healing in its wings. You shall go out leaping like calves from the stall" (Malachi 4:2).

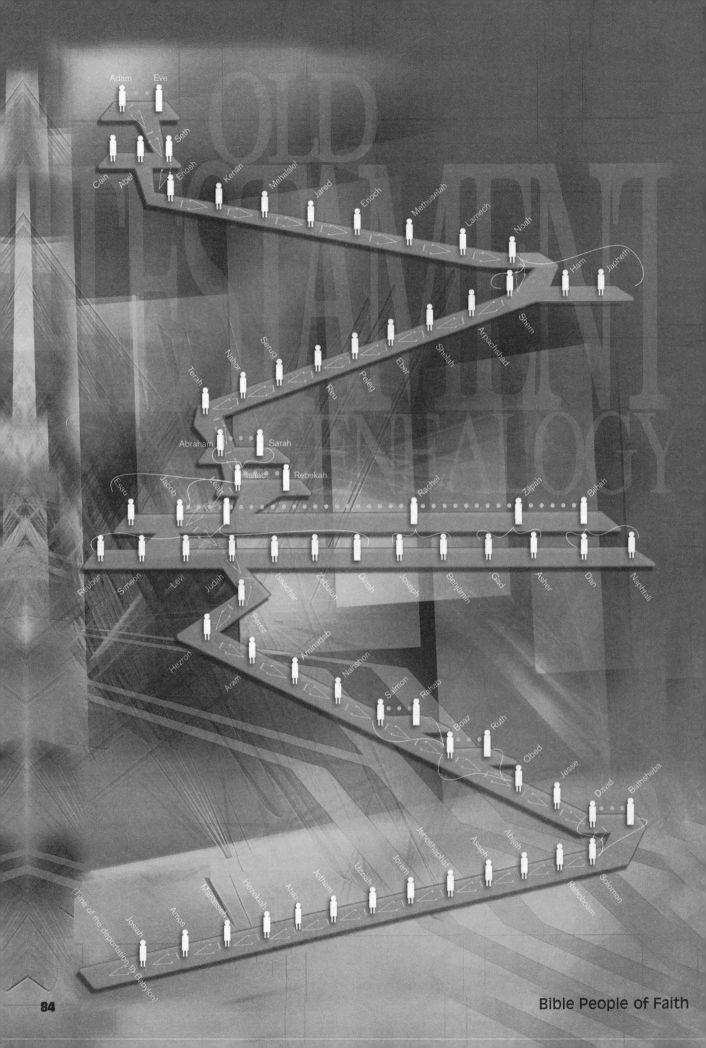

Adam Eve
Cain Abel Seth
Enosh Kenan Mahalalel Jared Enoch Methuselah Lamech Noah
Shem Ham Japheth
Arpachshad Shelah Eber Peleg Reu Serug Nahor Terah
Abraham Sarah
Isaac Rebekah
Esau Jacob Leah Rachel Zilpah Bilhah
Reuben Simeon Levi Judah Issachar Zebulun Dinah Joseph Benjamin Gad Asher Dan Naphtali
Perez Hezron Aram Aminadab Nahshon Salmon Rahab Boaz Ruth Obed Jesse David Bathsheba
Solomon Rehoboam Abijah Asaph Jehoshaphat Joram Uzziah Jotham Ahaz Hezekiah Manasseh Amos Josiah
(Time of the deportation to Babylon)

Bible People of Faith

DORCAS
- I am a Christian from the city of Joppa.
- My name means "gazelle."
- I am known for my acts of charity.
- Peter raised me from the dead.
- My name in Aramaic is "Tabitha."

ONESIMUS
- My name means "useful."
- I met Paul and was converted in Rome.
- I was sent to Philemon with a letter.
- I was a slave and had run away.
- Paul asked Philemon to set me free.

THE ETHIOPIAN EUNUCH
- I am in charge of the treasury.
- I am a high official in the court of a queen.
- I studied the Scriptures and asked a disciple for help with understanding them.
- I was baptized by Philip.
- I am from a country in Africa.

EUTYCHUS
- My name means "lucky" or "fortunate."
- I am from Troas.
- I went to a meeting where Paul spoke.
- Paul raised me from the dead.
- I went to sleep during a long sermon and fell out of a window.

RHODA
- I am a maid.
- My name means "rose."
- I work in the house of Mary, mother of John Mark.
- I answered a knock at the gate.
- I got excited and left Peter standing on the other side of a locked gate while I ran to tell the others he was there.

PRISCA / PRISCILLA
- I met Paul on his second missionary journey.
- I traveled a lot.
- My husband and I had to leave Rome because of an order from Claudius.
- I had influence in the church at Corinth.
- My husband is a tentmaker (or tanner) by trade.

CORNELIUS
- I am a Roman centurion in Caesarea.
- I am a "God-fearer."
- I am sometimes thought to be the first Gentile convert to Christianity.
- I saw a vision of an angel of the Lord telling me to go to Peter for help.
- Peter cured my servant.

AQUILA
- I met Paul on his second missionary journey.
- I traveled a lot.
- My wife and I had to leave Rome because of an order from Claudius.
- I had influence in the church at Corinth.
- I am a tentmaker (or tanner) by trade.

PHILEMON
- I am a Christian.
- I got a letter from Paul.
- I am a slave owner.
- My slave ran away.
- Paul asked that I set my slave free.

LYDIA
- I am from Thyatira.
- I am rich.
- I sell purple cloth.
- I was converted to Christianity by Paul.
- My entire household was baptized at the same time I was.

Bible People of Faith

JESUS

Life of Jesus

This is a very brief general overview of the life of Jesus.

Birth in Bethlehem (Matthew and Luke)   7/4 B.C.

Death of Herod the Great; return of Jesus' family to Nazareth   4 B.C.
    (Matthew)

Jesus at the Temple at the age of twelve (Luke)   Passover A.D. 5/8

John the Baptist begins ministry (Matthew, Mark, Luke, John)   A.D 25/29

Jesus is baptized in the Jordan River by John the Baptist
    (Matthew, Mark, Luke, John)

Jesus is tempted in the wilderness
    (Matthew, Mark, Luke)

Jesus begins his ministry   A.D. 26/27
    (Matthew, Mark, Luke)

Jesus calls his disciples, teaches, and performs miracles
    (Matthew, Mark, Luke, John)

The Final Week of Jesus' Life   A.D. 29/30
    Arrival at Bethany—Jesus sends two disciples to get a donkey
        (Matthew, Mark, Luke, John)
    Jesus triumphantly enters Jerusalem on a donkey (Matthew, Mark, Luke, John)   traditionally Sunday
    Jesus weeps over Jerusalem (Luke)
    Jesus curses the fig tree (Matthew, Mark)
    Jesus cleanses the Temple (Matthew, Mark, Luke) (John has this happening earlier in   Tuesday
        Jesus' ministry. He probably did this for theological reasons, establishing Jesus'
        authority as greater than that of the existing religious authority.)
    Jesus is anointed at Bethany by Mary (Matthew, Mark, John)
    Jeus washes the disciples' feet (John)
    Jesus has Passover with his disciples in the upper room
        (Matthew, Mark, Luke, John)   Thursday
    Jesus prays in the garden of Gethsemane (Matthew, Mark, Luke, John)   Thursday
    Jesus is arrested (Matthew, Mark, Luke, John)   Friday
    Jesus is tried (Matthew, Mark, Luke, John)   Friday
    Jesus is crucified (Matthew, Mark, Luke, John)   Friday
    Jesus is laid in the tomb (Matthew, Mark, Luke, John)   Friday
    Jesus is resurrected (Matthew, Mark, Luke, John)   Sunday
    Christ makes several post-Resurrection appearances (see page 94)
    Christ ascends to heaven (Mark, Luke, Acts)

JESUS

The Miracles of Jesus

	Matthew	Mark	Luke	John
Cleansing of a leper	8:1-4	1:40-45	5:12-16	
Healing of centurion's servant	8:5-13		7:1-10	
Healing of Peter's mother-in-law and many others	8:14-17	1:29-34	4:38-41	
Calming of the storm	8:23-27	4:35-41	8:22-25	
Curing of demon-possessed men	8:28-34	5:1-20	8:26-39	
Jesus heals a paralytic	9:1-8	2:1-12	5:17-26	
Jairus' daughter raised from dead	9:18-19, 23-26	5:21-24, 35-43	8:40-42, 49-56	
A woman healed (hemorrhages)	9:20-22	5:24-34	8:43-48	
Sight restored to two blind men	9:27-31			
Jesus heals a mute man	9:32-34			
The man with the withered hand	12:9-14	3:1-6	6:6-11	
Jesus cures mute demoniac	12:22		11:14	
Feeding of the five thousand	14:13-21	6:30-44	9:10-17	6:1-14
Jesus walks on water	14:22-33	6:45-52		6:15-21
Canaanite woman's daughter cured of demon	15:21-28	7:24-30		
Feeding of the four thousand	15:32-39	8:1-10		
Boy with demon cured	17:14-21	9:14-29	9:37-43a	
A coin in a fish's mouth (temple tax)	17:24-27			
Healing of blind Bartimaeus	20:29-34	10:46-52	18:35-43	
Jesus curses the fig tree	21:18-22	11:12-14, 20-25		
Man with an unclean spirit		1:21-28	4:31-37	
A deaf man is healed		7:31-37		
Blind man cured at Bethsaida		8:22-26		
Jesus calls first disciples with miraculous catch of fish			5:1-11	
Widow's son is raised at Nain			7:11-17	
Crippled woman healed			13:10-17	
Man with dropsy healed			14:1-6	
Ten lepers cleansed			17:11-19	
In Gethsemane Jesus restores ear			22:49-51	
Water changed into wine				2:1-11
Healing of official's son				4:46-54
Lame man healed at Beth-zatha pool				5:1-18
Healing of man born blind				9:1-12
Lazarus raised from the dead				11:1-45
Miraculous catch of fish (post-Resurrection)				21:1-14

The Parables of Jesus

A *parable* is a story that helps us understand a great truth. Jesus used parables to help us understand many things. (See use of parables in Matthew 13:10 and 13:34-35.) The meaning of many parables is abstract and needs interpretation, especially when used with children.

	Matthew	Mark	Luke
Kingdom Parables			
Sower and the Seed	13:1-8	4:1-9	8:4-8, 11-15
Weeds Among Wheat	13:24-30		
Mustard Seed	13:31-32	4:30-32	13:18-19
Yeast	13:33		13:20-21
Treasure	13:44		
Pearl of Great Price	13:45-46		
Net (Fishing)	13:47-50		
Growing Seed		4:26-29	
God's Love			
Lost Sheep	18:10-14		15:1-7
Lost Coin			15:8-10
Lost Son (Prodigal Son)			15:11-32
Two Debtors (Thankfulness)			7:41-43
Righteous Living			
The Unforgiving Servant	18:23-35		
Two Sons	21:28-32		
The Wicked Tenants	21:33-46	12:1-12	20:9-19
The Good Samaritan			10:30-37
Service/Obedience			
Laborers in the Vineyard	20:1-16		
Talents (Pounds)	25:14-30		19:11-27
Unworthy Servants			17:7-10
Prayer			
Friend at Midnight			11:5-8
The Widow and the Unjust Judge			18:1-8
Wealth			
The Rich Fool			12:13-21
The Dishonest Manager			16:1-9
Humility			
Lowest Place at the Banquet			14:7-11
Pharisee and the Tax Collector			18:9-14
Judgment and Future			
Parable of Wedding Banquet	22:1-14		14:15-24
Faithful and Unfaithful Slave	24:45-51		12:41-48
Ten Bridesmaids	25:1-13		
Watchful Doorkeeper		13:32-37	
Barren Fig Tree			13:6-9

Names and Titles of Jesus

This is a listing of some of the names and titles used for Jesus and by Jesus about himself.

Christ—Mark 1:1; Romans 15:5; 1 Corinthians 15:20 (more often: Jesus Christ or Christ Jesus)

King of kings—Revelation 17:14; 19:16

Lamb of God—John 1:29; 1 Corinthians 5:7; Revelation 5:6

Lord—Matthew 14:28; John 14:5; Acts 2:36

Lord of lords—Revelation 19:16

Messiah—Matthew 1:1-2; Luke 24:26; Acts 2:36

Son of David—Matthew 20:31; Matthew 21:9; Luke 18:38

Son of Man—Luke 19:10; John 1:51; Acts 7:56; Revelation 1:13 (self-designation most often used by Jesus)

Son of God (also, **the Son**)—John 3:35-36; Acts 9:20; Revelation 2:18

the Word (The Word of God)—John 1:1; Revelation 19:13

The "I Am" Sayings of Jesus

I am . . .

the bread of life (John 6:35)

the light of the world (John 8:12)

the gate for the sheep (John 10:7)

the good shepherd (John 10:11)

the resurrection and the life (John 11:25)

the way, the truth, and the life
(John 14:6)

the true vine (John 15:1)

the Alpha and the Omega, the first and the last, the beginning and the end
(Revelation 22:13)

the root and the descendant of David
(Revelation 22:16)

the bright morning star (Revelation 22:16)

Jesus' Post-Resurrection Appearances

Appeared to	Matthew	Mark	Luke	John	Acts	1 Corinthians
Mary Magdalene		16:9-11		20:1-18		
Mary Magdalene and other women	28:1-10	16:1	24:10			
Peter in Jerusalem			24:34			15:5
two men on the road to Emmaus		16:12-13	24:13-35			
the disciples in Jerusalem (behind closed doors)		16:14-18	24:36-43	20:19-23		
the disciples (including Thomas)				20:24-29		15:5
seven disciples by the Sea of Galilee				21:1-14		
eleven disciples on a mountain in Galilee	28:16-20					
a crowd of five hundred						15:6
James						15:7
the eleven disciples at the Ascension into heaven		16:19-20	24:50-53		1:6-11	

People
Jesus
Knew

Event: In-Church Progressive Dinner

Have a Christmas "progressive dinner." It works just like a regular progressive dinner with different courses in different places, but it takes place entirely on church property. The progression can be from one section to another in a large fellowship hall, or participants can progress to different classrooms or locations in the church. If you choose the latter, you may wish to have groups start at different intervals.

Each group in your church can make and serve something for the dinner. You may use the suggestions below or, better yet, come up with your own ideas.

PRESCHOOLERS Let guests visit the preschoolers last. The preschoolers can decorate either lunch bags or small gift bags with stickers or glue and glitter. Or they can decorate with their handprints dipped in paint. Each bag can contain candy and a homemade ornament made by the preschoolers. Provide each guest with one of these take-home treats.

EARLY ELEMENTARY Let early elementary children make a very simple dessert by icing ready-made sugar cookies and adding sprinkles to the cookies. Or make any dessert of your choice, and let the early elementary children serve the dessert to guests.

MIDDLE ELEMENTARY Have these children help make salad and plates of fruit. Plastic knives can be used so that middle elementary students can cut up bananas. They can wash grapes and strawberries. The children can also take bags of premade salad and mix them together, and set out plates, flatware, napkins and bottles of dressing. Then they can serve the salad to participants.

OLDER ELEMENTARY Purchase ready-to-bake rolls. Let older elementary children place the rolls on baking trays and brush them lightly with melted butter. Bake the bread. When it comes out of the oven (under supervision), have the children place the bread on plates or in baskets to serve. They can set tables with plates, knives, butter, and napkins. Have the children cut slices of cheese to serve with the bread.

TWEENS Let your fifth and sixth graders prepare and serve the main course (under supervision). A vegetable soup or stew would be easy for this group to prepare and serve.

YOUTH/ADULTS Ask for youth and adult volunteers to work with each age level of children to prepare and serve the meals. Ask other youth and adults to be the ones who progress through the meal as guests. Of course, be sure that at some point all the children have a chance to progress through the meal also. (They may take turns working and eating.)

MARY   *The mother of Jesus. The most blessed of women.*

We know little about this extremely important woman. Even when she is talked about in the Bible, there is very little information about her as a person.

According to Matthew and Luke, she was a young virgin living in Nazareth with her betrothed, Joseph. This was common since the betrothal was as official as marriage itself. At the end of her pregnancy with Jesus, she went with Joseph to Bethlehem, where her son was born. They later fled to Egypt to avoid Herod, who was looking for the Christ child.

Did Mary have other children? Matthew 12:46-50; 13:55-56; Mark 3:31-35; 6:3; Luke 8:19-21; John 2:12; and Acts 1:14 all mention brothers and/or sisters of Jesus. But does this make Mary their mother? Some say yes. Others say that since Joseph was much older than Mary, they were his children by another wife, a common practice of the time. Still others speculate that they were really Jesus' cousins.

Mary is mentioned only a few more times in the Bible. She was instrumental in Jesus' performing the miracle of turning water into wine at the wedding in Cana (John 2:1-11). She was also present at the foot of the cross, where Jesus put her in the care of the beloved disciple (John 19:25b-27).

The last reference to Mary in the Bible is in Acts 1:14. Mary, along with some of the disciples, certain women, as well as the brothers of Jesus, were gathered in Jerusalem.

There are many stories of Mary outside the Bible that circulated among the early church members.

JOSEPH   *Husband of Mary. Earthly father of Jesus.*

Very little is known of Joseph. What we do know is from the accounts of the birth and childhood of Jesus in Matthew and Luke. Both Gospels tell us that he was descended from the line of David. He was a carpenter (Matthew 13:55).

Matthew gives Joseph a large part in the birth narrative. It is in Matthew that Joseph, a righteous man, struggled with his conscience and was visited in a dream by an angel of the Lord. In Luke Joseph doesn't appear until he and Mary make the journey to Bethlehem to be registered for the census.

We know that Joseph took Jesus and his mother, Mary, to Egypt to escape the wrath of King Herod (Matthew 2:13-18) and returned with them after the death of Herod (Matthew 2:19-23). We know that Joseph was a faithful follower of the Law. He had Jesus circumcised (Luke 2:21), and he had the baby Jesus dedicated and offered a sacrifice for Mary's purification (Luke 2:22-24). Every year he took his family to Jerusalem to celebrate Passover (Luke 2:41). The last time we hear of Joseph is in Luke 2:41-52 when Jesus visited the Temple with his parents and stayed behind. Mary and Joseph were forced to go back to find him.

It is traditionally thought that Joseph died before Jesus started his ministry.

Event: Christmas Highlights

One night (or afternoon) in Advent, hold an event where reading children and/or youth and adults come to experience parts of the Christmas story.

CENSUS Have a church member make up a survey form to pass out, along with pencils, as participants enter. Before they can enter the room, they are to fill out their form and put it in a large, decorated box you have available at the door. You can do this survey according to your church's needs. You can have everyone fill out a form that will give the church some information it wants or needs such as birthdays, anniversaries, children's names, interests, and so forth, or you can make it like a census form. If you use the census form idea, then let them know they can make up answers. Have them register their location, number of family members (and pets), income, number of homes, and so forth.

NO ROOM Have a worship event, but purposely make the room crowded and the number of chairs fewer than the number of participants anticipated. Before the worship event ask everyone to please sit down. This should cause at least a little bit of scrambling to find a place to sit. Make sure everyone is seated before proceeding with worship. Some will have to sit on the floor.

VIEW THE MANGER Have some carpenters in your church help you build a manger if you don't have one that is life-size already. Have kids volunteer to be animals and make animal masks that they can hold in front of their faces. Have them practice making animal sounds beforehand. Have actors mime the parts of the characters as the Christmas story is read. You may wish to have everyone view this at one time or come in groups to the manger while others do the "Posting Wall" activity. Then reverse the groups. Or if you have a lot of people coming to this event, use "Census," "No Room," "View the Manger," and "Posting Wall" as centers with these things going on simultaneously and continuously. People can then rotate through the centers at specified intervals.

POSTING WALL Provide a large wall or bulletin boards and supplies. Ask people to write something that expresses their feelings about the Christmas season and/or something they have experienced at this event. They can do this through a short sentence, single words, a drawing, a poem, or whatever expresses the way they feel.

Encourage people to visit the wall more than once so that they can see what others have posted.

ZECHARIAH AND ELIZABETH *Parents of John the Baptist.*

Zechariah was a priest (Luke 1:5) and Elizabeth was related to Mary, the mother of Jesus (Luke 1:36).

Like many other biblical couples, they were older and could not have children. One day during Zechariah's priestly duties, the angel Gabriel appeared to him to deliver the news that the couple would have a child that would be great in the sight of the Lord. Zechariah expressed skepticism, and for this he was struck mute until the day his son was born (Luke 1:5-23, 57-66).

It was to Elizabeth that Mary went with the great news of the child she was to bear.

When Zechariah and Elizabeth's son, John, was born, Zechariah regained his voice. He uttered a beautiful prophecy of messianic hope for Israel (Luke 1:67-79).

SIMEON AND ANNA *Simeon was a righteous and devout man in Jerusalem. The Holy Spirit touched him and promised that he would not die before he saw the Messiah.*

Simeon was guided to the Temple by the Holy Spirit on the day that Jesus was brought by his parents to be dedicated. Simeon held the baby Jesus in his arms and offered a prayer of praise to God.

Simeon then gave a prophecy to Mary that there would be much opposition to her son and that she too would suffer because of this: "A sword will pierce your own soul too." Simeon's story is in Luke 2:22-35.

Anna was a prophet. She was eighty-four years old at the time of Jesus' birth. Anna never left the Temple. She worshiped, fasted, and prayed night and day.

When Jesus was brought to the Temple for his dedication, Anna was there and began to praise God. Her story is told in Luke 2:36-38.

Activity: Make a Crèche Display

Make one or more Nativity sets to display for the entire church this year and perhaps for years to come. Choose one or more (perhaps all) of the suggested methods below, depending upon ages involved in construction of the display.

While we know that the wise men did not come to the manger but rather to the two-year-old Jesus in a house, it is traditional to put the wise men at the manger scene. This helps to complete the story of the birth of Jesus and the flight into Egypt. Include the wise men in your display.

SILHOUETTE NATIVITY Tape a large sheet of paper (the kind that comes in rolls) to a wall. Ask a participant to stand in front of the paper. Dim the lights and use a spotlight or flashlight to create a shadow of the person onto the paper. Ask the person to take a stance as one of the people of the Nativity story. Trace the outline of the person onto the paper. Cut around the figure created. Tape or glue it to a large sheet of cardboard and have participants color in the figure, being sure to give it a face. Repeat until you have a full Nativity.

To make this more special and longer lasting, ask a woodworker in your congregation to use the paper patterns you created and cut the figures out of cardboard. Then have participants paint the figures. You might even wish to make clothing for the figures out of cloth.

Either way, remember to make a stand for each figure, using more cardboard or wood attached to the back of each figure.

CLAY NATIVITY Give each participant a hunk of clay. Assign them one of the people (or animals) in the Nativity story, and let them fashion it out of clay. After the clay dries, have them paint the figures. You may use self-drying clay or the type that needs to be baked.

PAINTED GLASSES NATIVITY Buy an inexpensive but sturdy set of clear drinking glasses. Have an artist in your church make patterns out of paper for each Nativity figure. Ask participants to use one of the patterns to trace a Nativity figure onto one glass. Provide paints that work well on glass, and have participants paint in the figures they have outlined.

NOTE: You may wish to combine the activities on pages 96, 98, and 100 to make one big, spectacular event. For a small church it could even be a good substitute for the Sunday morning worship and Sunday school time when Sunday falls on Christmas Eve or Christmas Day.

JOHN THE BAPTIST
Son of the priest Zechariah and his wife, Elizabeth. A prophet. A cousin of Jesus, six months older than Jesus (Luke 1:36).

Though his father was a priest, John seemed to model himself after Elijah. He wore clothing made of camel's hair with a leather belt. He ate food such as locusts and honey. Most people feel that if he modeled himself after Elijah, he would also have let his hair and beard grow (2 Kings 1:8).

John the Baptist was well known and had a large following of disciples. John was so well known that Josephus, the historian, tells his story (though with perhaps a different interpretation from that of the Bible).

While there were some groups that used a form of ablution, their reason and meaning were different. John's form of baptism was unique. The baptism John performed was a symbolic rebirth, a symbol of repentance, of washing away sin that brought salvation. Mark tells us that baptism involved the forgiveness of sins (Mark 1:5).

Jesus himself came to John to be baptized, though John protested that he was the one who needed to be baptized by Jesus (Matthew 3:13-17).

John's arrest was associated with the beginning of Jesus' ministry (Mark 1:14-15).

John was executed by Herod Antipas (a descendant of Herod the Great). Herod had been angered by John's denunciation of his marriage to Herodias as being illegal according to the Hebrew law. Herodias' daughter danced at a banquet and was promised a reward. She asked for John the Baptist's head on a platter and was rewarded with the head, which she took to her mother (Matthew 14:1-12 and Mark 6:14-29).

Outline of John's Life

- An aging Zechariah is told by Gabriel, an angel of the Lord, that he and his wife, Elizabeth, will have the son they have longed for, and that he will be great in the sight of the Lord. Because of his disbelief, Zechariah is struck dumb until John is born (Luke 1: 5-23, 57-66).

- Zechariah prophesies John's role as the forerunner to the Messiah (Luke 1:67-79).

- John is in the wilderness until his ministry begins and he appears in public (Luke 1:80).

- John the Baptizer appears in the wilderness, proclaiming a baptism of repentance for forgiveness of sins. He becomes popular and has a great following. He proclaims that one more powerful than himself will come (Matthew 3:1-12; Mark 1:1-8; Luke 3:1-20; John 1:19-28).

- John the Baptizer baptizes Jesus (Matthew 3:13-17; Mark 1:9-11; Luke 3:21-22; John 1:29-34).

- John is arrested and Jesus begins his Galilean ministry (Mark 1:14-15).

- John is executed by Herod Antipas. John's head is presented to Herodias on a platter (Matthew 14:1-12; Mark 6:14-29; Luke 9:7-9).

Event: Remembering Your Baptism

This event is for sixth graders through adults. Younger children do not have the abstract thought processes to go deeply enough into the topic. While what they say may sound good, most of it will be things they have heard but not fully processed. Take this time to help your sixth graders who are ready to take on church membership responsibilities to think more deeply about their baptism, hopefully with the participation of adults and youth.

READ THE STORY Divide participants into four groups. Assign each group one of the Gospel accounts of Jesus' baptism: Matthew 3:13-17; Mark 1:9-11; Luke 3:21-22; and John 1:29-34. Ask the groups to be prepared to answer questions about their version.

Post each question on a large sheet of paper and make four columns—one for each Gospel. Ask each group to write their answers to the questions on the large sheet of paper.

- Where was Jesus baptized?
- Who baptized Jesus?
- Who was present?
- What happened when Jesus was baptized?
- What did God say about Jesus?

(Please note that some groups will have questions they cannot answer. They are to leave those spaces blank.)

Go over answers together. Talk about the importance of the event being recorded in all four Gospels. Discuss likenesses and differences. Remind participants that when people report on the same event they usually report on those things that are most important to them.

TELL YOUR STORY Provide opportunities for people to talk about their baptism. If you have tweens who have been baptized, they might have been too young to remember it. If there are family members present, encourage them to talk about their tween's baptism and what it meant to them. Older siblings who were present might wish to share also. Ask any present who wish to do so to tell what they remember or have been told about their own baptism.

LOOK AT BAPTISMAL LANGUAGE Bring copies of your church's baptism ritual to the session. Encourage participants to share what the words mean to them.

SYMBOLIZE YOUR BAPTISM Provide various craft materials. Speak of how the shell with three drops of water symbolizes baptism by the Father, Son, and Holy Spirit. Have participants work individually or in small groups to come up with a baptism symbol that expresses how they feel about their baptism. Let participants or groups share their symbols.

PETER

*Simon Bar Jonah (son of Jonah). He was given the name **Cephas** (Aramaic) or **Petros** (Greek meaning **rock**). It is from **Petros** that we get the name **Peter**. A Galilean fisherman. Brother of Andrew. Husband [he has a mother-in-law (Luke 4:38)]. The first and most well known of the twelve disciples.*

Peter was part of Jesus' inner circle, which also included James and John. These three often went with Jesus for important occasions, such as the Transfiguration. Peter is sometimes known for changing his position. The best-known example of this is when, upon the arrest of Jesus, Peter knowingly betrayed Jesus three times. Peter seems to have been so devastated by his betrayal of Jesus that he never again wavered in his faith.

Even though Jesus knew that Peter would and did betray him, his faith in Peter was strong. It was Peter that Jesus entrusted to build his church; it was Peter to whom he gave the "keys of the kingdom of heaven" (Matthew 16:17-19); and it was to Peter he entrusted the care of the faithful, even though this would bring Peter to death (John 21:15-19).

It was Peter who would lead the church after the death, resurrection, and ascension of Jesus. It was Peter who addressed the crowd at Pentecost. Though Peter and Paul would clash over various issues, both remained faithful to Christ and his earthly church, even though it cost both of them their lives.

After the death of Jesus, Peter the vacillator did indeed prove himself to be the "rock" on which Christ built the church.

Some Main Events of Peter's Story

- Peter is called to be a disciple (Matthew 4:18-20; Mark 1:16-20; Luke 5:1-11).

- Peter attempts to walk on water to Jesus, but his faith fails, and Jesus has to catch him (Matthew 14:22-32).

- Peter declares his faith that Jesus is the Messiah, the Son of the living God, and Jesus names him the "rock" on whom he will build his church and to whom he will give the keys to the kingdom (Matthew 16:13-20; Mark 8:27-30; Luke 9:18-20).

- Peter is with Jesus at the Transfiguration (Matthew 17:1-13; Mark 9:2-13; Luke 9:28-36, 2 Peter 1:16-18).

- Peter is with Jesus at the Last Supper. His denial of Jesus is foretold (Matthew 26:31-35; Mark 14:27-31; Luke 22:31-34; John 13:36-38).

- Peter, James, and John are with Jesus in the garden of Gethsemane (Matthew 26:36-46; Luke 22:39-46).

- Peter denies Jesus three times before the cock crows (Matthew 26:69-75; Mark 14:66-72; Luke 22:54-62; John 18:15-18, 25-27).

- Peter runs to the tomb when he hears of the Resurrection (John 20:2-10).

- Peter is present at several post-Resurrection appearances (see listing of appearances on page 94).

- Peter is charged with taking care of the believers (John 21:15-19).

- Peter delivers the first sermon (Acts 2:14-36).

- Peter heals and teaches (Acts 3–4; 9:36-43; 10–11).

- Peter has a vision interpreted as meaning that the good news should be taken to the Gentiles (Acts 10).

- Peter is imprisoned and later is freed by an angel (Acts 12).

- Peter writes letters to the faithful (First and Second Peter).

- Tradition says Peter was a martyr for his faith. He requested to be crucified upside down because he did not feel worthy of dying the same way Jesus did.

Event: Here I Am, Lord!

This intergenerational stewardship study (pages 104, 106, and 108) is designed to be used with tweens (10-13 years old) through adults. If you wish, you can modify or add events for middle and older elementary children. You may wish to do this study over several sessions.

When joining the church, we are often asked if we will support the church through our prayers, our presence, our gifts, and our service. These same commitments need to be made to all forms of discipleship. This event is designed to center on these four areas of service.

PRAYER As participants arrive, divide them into individuals or groups to start through the prayer centers you have set up around the fellowship hall or other large room. Have printed instructions posted in each center. There are four centers:

SELF—Have index cards and pens and pencils available. Have a "prayer box"
(a shoebox works well) that has a lid with a slot cut in the top.
Instructions:
Think of one thing you would like to talk to God about. Write it on an index card and put the card in the prayer box. No one else will see your prayer.
CHURCH—Have a large sheet of paper taped to the wall and markers available.
Instructions:
Think of one concern you have about your local church that you would like to speak with God about. Write that concern on the posted paper. Now say a prayer to God for every concern you see on the paper.
THE WORLD—Have index cards, pens, pencils, and tape available. Have a world map posted on the wall.
Instructions:
Think of one thing about the world and all the people in it that you would like to talk to God about. Write it on an index card and tape it on the wall close to the world map. Now say a prayer for your concern.
LISTENING FOR GOD—Have soft, prayerful music continuously playing in this center. Have a clock in the center.
Instructions:
Sit quietly for two full minutes. Do not pray. Do not talk. Take deep breaths and then slowly let each breath out. Try not to think of anything, if that's possible. Give God a chance to speak to your heart.

PRESENCE After everyone has had a chance to go through the prayer centers, bring all participants together for a corporate worship experience. Use music, symbols, and prayers as part of the worship. The length of the worship will be dictated by how long your event will be.

Either at the beginning or end of your worship experience, explain to participants that individual prayer brings us closer to God. Corporate worship helps us maintain our relationship to the family of God.

JUDAS ISCARIOT

*Judas was a common name in biblical times. Many attempts have been made to assign a meaning to **Iscariot**. Some have even tried to make it fit the word **assassin**. Though we do not know for sure, many scholars feel that the name **Iscariot** actually refers to Judas' hometown, which may have been Kerioth. For modern people Judas' name has come to be used to mean **betrayer**.*

Judas was called by Jesus to be one of the twelve disciples. From the time of his call until Jesus neared the end of his ministry and his life, we do not hear from Judas again.

When we do hear of Judas, it is during the final days of Jesus' life. And all four Gospels tell his story, though we get different details from them. According to John 12:6 and 13:29, Judas was the treasurer of the disciples. John 12:6 also tells us that Judas was a thief.

Jesus predicted that one of the disciples (and some of the Gospels seem to single out Judas for this role) would betray him. Judas did betray Jesus and was paid thirty pieces of silver (Matthew 26:14-16). It seems he was paid to deliver Jesus to the chief priests at a time and place where Jesus would be isolated from the crowds, and there would be little resistance.

There are two accounts of Judas' death (see below).

Some Main Events of Judas' Story

- Called to be a disciple (Matthew 10:4; Mark 3:19; Luke 6:16).

- Six days before the Passover (the Last Supper), Judas complains when Mary of Bethany anoints Jesus' feet with costly perfume. He says the money could have been given to the poor (John 12:1-8).

- Judas goes to the chief priests and agrees to betray Jesus for thirty pieces of silver (Matthew 26:14-16).

- At the Last Supper Jesus reveals that he will be betrayed by someone sitting at the table with him (Matthew 26:20-25; Mark 14:17-21; Luke 22:14, 21-23).

- After receiving the piece of bread, Satan enters Judas, who leaves the meal (John 13:27-30).

- After praying in the garden, Jesus is speaking with the disciples when Judas arrives with a large crowd, including the chief priests and the elders. Judas betrays Jesus with a kiss (Matthew 26:47-50).

- Judas repents of his sin, taking the thirty pieces of silver to the chief priests and the elders. He throws down the pieces of silver in the Temple. He leaves and goes and hangs himself. A potter's field is purchased with the money (Matthew 27:3-10).

OR

- Judas purchases a field with his thirty pieces of silver. He falls headlong in the field and bursts open and dies (Acts 1:18-19). The field becomes known as the "Field of Blood."

Event: Here I Am, Lord!—Part 2

GIFTS The following two activities are to help people focus on the two important things about gifts that disciples need to make part of their response to God in their lives—money and personal response to God.

MONEY—Post a sheet of newsprint or use a markerboard. If you have a large number of participants, you may divide them into groups, each completing their own list on separate sheets of newsprint. Ask participants to brainstorm as many ways as they can that people get money (legitimately). (*Some possibilities: work, allowance, bonus, gift, inheritance*)

Divide participants into three groups. Assign each group one of these Bible stories: Mark 12:41-44—The Widow's Mite; Luke 18:9-14—Pharisee and Tax Collector; Luke 18:18-25—Rich Young Ruler. Ask each group to be prepared to act out their story for the others, to give a synopsis of what they learned from their story, or to retell the story.

Bring all groups back together and have volunteers read aloud: Genesis 14:20b; Genesis 28:20-22; and 2 Chronicles 31:5.

Have participants then debate whether or not tithing should come from all the categories they earlier brainstormed. Be sure that participants understand that the Bible is unclear, but that many churches understand tithe is to come from our basic income. However, the important thing is that tithing helps us understand that everything we have comes from God. Individual decisions have to be made about what that means.

GIFTS AND TALENTS—To be a good disciple we must give of ourselves to the common good of fellow Christians and to others.
- Depending upon your time frame, arrange with a group beforehand to act out Acts 6:1-7—Seven Chosen to Serve the Church. Or prepare to read the story aloud for participants.
- Immediately after the story preparation, ask a volunteer to read Romans 12:3-8. Ask another volunteer to read Romans 12:13.
- Divide participants into groups and ask them to work together to complete the "Gifts and Talents" survey (page 108) for each member of their group. (Sometimes other people are better at recognizing our talents than we are.)
- Have groups talk together about how each person could do one thing for the church community that would use their gifts and talents. The group can propose several things, but only the individual can make the final decision, and that decision does NOT have to be shared with the group.

SERVICE To complete your stewardship study, have participants take part in a service project where using their gifts and talents in a joint venture is important. Contact local agencies to find an important need in your area.

ANDREW *(meaning* **manly** *in Greek) Simon Peter's brother. The brothers were fishermen. Andrew is thought to have first been a disciple of John the Baptist, who told him about Jesus. Andrew introduced his brother, Simon Peter, to Jesus. Andrew is best remembered for his great role in bringing others to Jesus (John 1:35-42).*

Tradition says that Andrew was martyred in Greece, requesting to die on an X-shaped cross because he felt unworthy to die on the same kind of cross that Jesus died on.

BARTHOLOMEW *(or Nathanael—meaning* **gift of God***). Often Bartholomew and Nathanael are thought to be the same person. Bartholomew is a* patronymic *(last name).*

At first Nathanael was skeptical of Jesus until Jesus told Nathanael a lot of things about him that Jesus would have had no way of knowing. This impressed him (John 1:43-51).

Tradition says that Bartholomew (Nathanael) traveled extensively as a missionary to places such as Egypt, Persia, India, and Armenia. It is said that he was put to death in Armenia.

JUDAS SON OF JAMES *(or Thaddaeus) Luke's Gospel calls this disciple* **Judas son of James.** *In the Book of Mark, he is called* **Thaddaeus;** *and in some older texts he is called* **Lebbeus.** *This is one explanation given as to the reason why there are different listings for the names of the twelve disciples.*

Tradition says that Judas son of James (Thaddaeus) traveled extensively as a missionary.

MATTHEW *A tax collector. His name appears in every list of the disciples. It was Jesus himself who called Matthew to join the disciples (Matthew 9:9-13). Matthew left his old ways behind (tax collectors were able to do a lot of skimming off the top to support themselves) and followed Jesus. This Matthew is traditionally considered to be the author of the Gospel According to Matthew.*

Activity: Gifts and Talents Survey

Below number in order things you like to do (with one being the thing you like the most).

____ animals

____ anything I can do with friends

____ cooking

____ crafts

____ drama and plays

____ e-mailing

____ flowers

____ gardening

____ making videos

____ organizing

____ painting/home repair

____ people

____ playing an instrument

____ playing games

____ PowerPoint

____ power tools

____ reading

____ repairing things

____ service projects

____ sewing

____ singing

____ taking care of people

____ talking in front of people

____ traveling

____ woodworking

____ working with sound/lighting equipment

____ _____

____ _____

Three things I am good at:

1. _____

2. _____

3. _____

Three things the group thinks I'm good at:

1. _____

2. _____

3. _____

Bible People of Faith

PHILIP *First Christian missionary. After Philip was called to be a disciple by Jesus, he went and told his friend Nathanael (Bartholomew, see page 107) that he had found the one "about whom Moses in the law and also the prophets wrote" (John 1:45).*

In the story of the feeding of the five thousand, it was Philip who responded to Jesus' question about how they were to feed the crowds by saying, "Six months' wages would not buy enough bread for each of them to get a little" (John 6:7).

SIMON THE ZEALOT *He was probably called* **the Zealot** *either because of his political or his religious views. (We are not sure which.)*

Some people feel that since Simon was called **the Zealot**, *he might have had a rather violent nature that was drawn to Jesus' talk of a "new kingdom," mistaking it for a new "earthly" kingdom free from the Romans. However, there is no way to be sure how Simon felt.*

Simon was also called the **Cananaean**, *which was an early name for those who later came to be called* **Zealots**.

THOMAS *(meaning* **twin***). We do not know who Thomas' twin was. The only major statement or story about Thomas is in the Gospel of John. In this story Thomas asks for proof of Jesus' resurrection. This story gave him the name* **Doubting Thomas**, *even though after shown the proof he did indeed believe (John 20:24-29).*

Tradition says that Thomas went to India and built a church with his own hands. Thomas was believed to have been martyred by being stabbed with a spear.

JAMES SON OF ALPHAEUS *Also known as* **James the Younger** *(Mark 15:40) or* **James the Little***. It is speculated that this means that he was probably shorter than James the Greater, thus the* **younger** *or* **little** *designation.*

Tradition says that James was martyred by being thrown from the top of a church and his body then sawed into pieces.

Activity: People of Holy Week Worship

Dramatize by word and symbol what happened during Holy Week.

Have an altar or worship table on which to place symbols. Set an empty cross on the altar. Assign parts. As each person speaks (using cards from this page and page 112), have him or her follow the directions on the card. After *Simon of Cyrene* speaks, have all characters come in silence and remove all of the symbols from the altar. Then return to speakers, following directions on their cards.

(1) DISCIPLE ONE   (Matthew 21:1-11)

I am one of two disciples that Jesus sent to bring the donkey and the colt to carry him into Jerusalem. What a great day that was with all the cheering of the crowds and the palm branches and the cloaks that were thrown before him as he rode!

We all thought then that at last everyone would recognize him and proclaim him as king. He had tried to warn us, but we wanted to believe that this praise would continue.

Place a palm branch on the altar.

(2) BLIND MAN   (Matthew 21:12-17)

Things got pretty interesting the day that Jesus cleansed the Temple. I couldn't see, but I heard him say, "'My house shall be called a house of prayer'; but you are making it a den of robbers."

I heard the crack of a whip as the money changers and dove sellers were run out of the Temple. The noise of overturning tables and squawking doves was unbelievable.

Jesus restored my sight that day, but the chief priests were angry because they thought he had no right to act this way in the house of God.

Place a stack of coins on the altar.

(3) MARTHA   (John 12:1-8)

At our house my sister, Mary, took a pound of costly perfume and anointed the feet of Jesus, wiping his feet with her hair. You should have heard Judas complain about the cost and the poor, as if he ever cared about the poor. I was heartbroken when Jesus said, "You always have the poor with you, but you do not always have me."

Place a perfume bottle on the altar.

(4) DISCIPLE TWO   (Matthew 26:17-30)

I will always remember that last Passover meal in the upper room. Jesus washed our feet, showing us that we are meant to be servants of others.

After telling us that one of us would betray him, that shocked us and disturbed us. None of us wanted to believe that we were capable of such a thing.

Then Jesus gave us the first Communion. We still use this Communion to keep Jesus in our hearts.

Place a cup and plate on the altar.

(5) JOHN   (Matthew 26:36-46)

I couldn't stay awake in the garden as Jesus prayed, no matter how hard I tried. I was grieved at his disappointment in us.

Place a flower on the altar.

JAMES *the greater. James (the greater or the elder) was one of the sons of Zebedee—brother of John, the beloved disciple. Together with John and Peter, James formed the inner circle of Jesus' disciples. The three were often with Jesus for significant events, even when the other disciples were absent.*

James and John were nicknamed **Sons of Thunder***. Many people believe that they had volatile tempers. James is most often referred to in the New Testament, along with his brother and/or with Peter. We know almost nothing about him.*

James was the first of the twelve disciples to be martyred for his faith (Acts 12:1-2). Remember that Judas Iscariot committed suicide; he was not a martyr.

JOHN *Son of Zebedee, brother of James the greater. The disciple "whom Jesus loved" (John 13:23). While the beloved disciple is not named, most biblical scholars agree it was John, the son of Zebedee.*

John, along with his brother James and Peter, formed the inner circle around Jesus. John was so close to Jesus that while he was on the cross, Jesus entrusted his mother to John's care (John 19:25-27).

John and James are the brothers who fought over who would sit at the right or left hand of Jesus in the Kingdom (Mark 10:35-45). Jesus' answer shows that "being part of the in-group" may not get you too far in the kingdom of heaven. God has a whole different set of criteria.

There is a legend that once John was given a cup of poisoned wine to drink. John made the sign of the cross over the chalice, and the poison became a serpent and crawled away. John is the only disciple other than Thaddaeus who escaped a martyr's death. Tradition has it that John lived many years.

MARY MAGDALENE *This Mary is identified by the town from which she comes. Magdala is thought to be on the west side of the Sea of Galilee, north of Tiberias. Luke 8:2 tells us that Jesus had cured her of seven demons. She is named as one of many women followers of Jesus. These women disciples helped support his ministry financially.*

There is no reason to believe from any biblical accounts of Mary that she was the sinful woman mentioned in Luke 7:36-50. *If she were, why would Luke introduce her as if for the first time in 8:2? There is no biblical indication at all that states that Mary was a prostitute. That is a later church tradition.*

While Luke constantly shows us that women followers were important to Jesus' ministry, Mary Magdalene was really only shown in importance at the Crucifixion and Resurrection. A sign of her importance is that all four Gospels place her at the cross and at the Resurrection itself. At the Crucifixion other women are also named. In the Resurrection story Mary Magdalene is given a significant role. Everything else about Mary Magdalene comes from sources, traditions, or theories outside the Bible.

(6) JUDAS (Matthew 26:14-16, 20-25, 47-50; 27:3-10)

I can't believe I committed such a terrible sin. Jesus knew I was going to do it. Why didn't he stop me? It wasn't for the money. Thirty pieces of silver even then wasn't a lot of money. I thought I could force him to declare himself as earthly ruler instead of acting like being king on this earth didn't matter. I just didn't understand. If I had, would I still have betrayed him? I don't know. I killed myself because I betrayed the most wonderful man I ever knew.

Take a pouch of coins and **empty** them onto the altar.

(7) PETER (Matthew 26:69-75)

I can't believe that I denied I knew him. He told me I would. I was so sure I wouldn't. I was so scared that they would arrest and kill me. When that servant girl said I had been with Jesus, I just opened my mouth and said that I didn't know what she was talking about. And then to make matters worse, I did it twice more, right before the cock crowed three times.

That was the last time I ever denied Jesus. I never will again, no matter what they do to me.

Place a clock on the altar.

(8) CHIEF PRIEST (Matthew 26:47–27:2)

Jesus was a troublemaker. He blasphemed against God, pretending that he was the Messiah. With Rome in control we were in a bad position. If there were trouble among the Jews, Rome would come down on us hard. If this Jesus managed to start a rebellion, a lot of Jewish people could end up dead. We had a responsibility. We did what we had to do to protect the people.

Besides, he was betrayed by one of his own. Who would betray his own Messiah? We might as well put this blood money to good use.

Pick up some coins from the altar.

9) PILATE (Matthew 27:1-14)

I'm fed up with these troublesome Jews. If they want to kill him, I wash my hands of the whole mess.

Place a basin and towel on the altar.

(10) SIMON OF CYRENE (Mark 15:21)

My sons, Alexander and Rufus, believed in Jesus. I was forced to carry his cross.

Take the empty cross from the altar and hand it to the *Centurion* (person who speaks next).

(11) CENTURION AT THE CROSS (Matthew 27:45-56)

I was a Roman that scoffed at this petty criminal, this Jesus, the so-called "King of the Jews." That is, I scoffed until at the moment of his death when the sky turned dark, the curtain of the temple was torn in two, and the earth shook from a quake. That scared me! That was when I said, "Truly this man was God's Son!"

Place the empty cross back on the altar.

(12) JOSEPH OF ARIMATHEA (Matthew 27:57-61; John 19:39)

According to the law, Jesus had to be buried the same day he died. I had an empty tomb on land that I had purchased when I moved to Jerusalem.

I moved his body and buried it. I was helped by Nicodemus the Pharisee, who brought myrrh and aloes for the body.

Drape the cross with a white cloth.

(13) MARY MAGDALENE (Matthew 28:1-10)

I, along with other women, discovered the empty tomb. You can imagine how my overwhelming grief turned to unimaginable joy when I saw Jesus for myself! I ran as fast as I could to report the news.

Place a flower before the draped cross on the altar.

(14) DOUBTING THOMAS (John 20:24-29)

It shames me to tell of it, but I just couldn't believe in the Resurrection until I actually touched the wounds in Jesus' side. While it made me happy, to this day I wish I had been like the others and believed without proof. He has risen! Jesus lives! Jesus brings the joy of eternal life.

Pin a paper butterfly to the cloth on the cross.

MARTHA *(meaning **lady**) Friend of Jesus. Sister of Mary of Bethany and Lazarus.*

We all know the story of Martha trying to carry out her duties as hostess while Mary sat at the feet of Jesus. When Martha asked Jesus for support, he told her she worried too much, that Mary had chosen the better part (Luke 10:38-42).

When her brother, Lazarus, became ill (John 11:1-44), Martha and her sister sent a message to Jesus. Jesus delayed arriving. Martha told Jesus that if he had been there, Lazarus would not have died. However, she went on to express that God would give Jesus whatever he asked. Her statement, "Yes, Lord, I believe that you are the Messiah, the Son of God, the one coming into the world," is one of the first statements of belief.

Martha's third and final appearance was at her house in Bethany when Mary anointed Jesus' feet. Of course, as usual, it was Martha who was serving (John 12:2).

MARY OF BETHANY *Friend of Jesus. Sister of Martha and Lazarus.*

Mary sat at the feet of Jesus, eager to learn (Luke 10:38-42). After Jesus raised her brother, Lazarus, from the dead, a dinner was served to Jesus. It was at this dinner that Mary anointed Jesus' feet with costly oil. This was an emotional response given with great devotion. Judas Iscariot was upset about the use of the money, but Jesus understood the gesture and was grateful. Mary is known for her great devotion to Jesus (John 12:1-8).

LAZARUS *Friend of Jesus. Brother of Martha and Mary. This is all we really know about Lazarus except for his dying and being brought back to life by Jesus.*

Jesus must truly have loved this friend for he wept at his tomb. However, he had delayed his arrival when he heard that Lazarus was ill. Why? Jesus said, "This illness does not lead to death; rather it is for God's glory." Jesus called for Lazarus to come out of the tomb. Later Lazarus was at the meal celebrating his being brought back from the dead.

In John 12:9-11 we learn that the chief priests planned to put Lazarus to death because his resurrection was causing many to believe in Jesus. This was the beginning of the plot against Jesus. Strangely, this is the last we hear of Lazarus.

Activity: Fruit of the Spirit Fun

Use the "Fruit of the Spirit Scripture" to reinforce Christian values. After any of the activities, read Galatians 5:22-23a and 5:25-26.

Photocopy and cut apart the cards on page 116. You may choose to use these cards in one or more of the following ways:

Illustration Ask participants to draw one of the cards out of a basket or other container. Provide craft supplies. Ask them to illustrate their "Fruit of the Spirit" in art (*drawing a cartoon, writing a poem, drawing stick figures, doing an abstract painting, or making a figure from clay*). When finished, let them display their work, and those who wish to do so can explain their art. This may be done as individuals or in groups.

Double Charades Divide participants into two groups. Play charades with a twist. Each group will send forward one member to act out a word. The team member for both teams will be given the same word. They will start at exactly the same time to act out the word for their group. The group that guesses the word first gets a point.

Throw in a couple of extra words to make it more challenging in case someone knows all the "Fruit of the Spirit" words (*possibilities: happy, fun, caring*).

Fruit of the Spirit Challenge Divide your participants into groups of nine. If you do not have enough participants to do that, then give each group more than one word. Just be sure that the number of words is equal.

Give each group five minutes to come up with as many ways as they can think of that they can demonstrate that "Fruit of the Spirit" in their daily lives. (*For example: Faithfulness—pray for others, read the Bible, choose not to take drugs, be kind to someone who has been mean to them, and so forth*)

Bring the groups back together and let each read their list.
Score as follows:
- One point for each item on list that doesn't repeat.
- Five points for something really creative.
- Ten points for members who can HONESTLY say they have done three things on their list this week.

NOTE: People, especially kids, love competition. Instead of fighting it, use competition to help people learn. By working in groups you also teach teamwork.

ZACCHAEUS *Chief tax collector of Jericho.*

That he was the chief tax collector meant he probably had other tax collectors under him. Tax collectors were allowed to tax whatever amount they could get. A set portion of the tax would go to occupying Romans. He was rich, which probably meant that he had overcharged a lot. Because of his position and character, he was hated by the average hard-working person.

Zacchaeus was short. In fact, he was so short he had to climb a tree in order to see Jesus.

The crowd was not happy with Jesus when he went to the home of Zacchaeus. But Zacchaeus' conversion experience was so heartfelt that it had practical results. He vowed to restore more than he had defrauded.

Zacchaeus' salvation was not only for himself, but for his whole household. Jesus tells us at the end of the story why he ministered to Zacchaeus and all like him. "The Son of Man came to seek out and to save the lost." Read Zacchaeus' story in Luke 19:1-10.

JOANNA *One of many women who followed Jesus. These women provided for Jesus and the disciples out of their own resources.*

Joanna was the wife of Chuza, the steward of Herod Antipas. Jesus cured her of some illness (Luke 8:2-3), but Luke is the only Gospel to tell her story. She was at the cross when Jesus was crucified (Luke 23:49, 55). She was also at the tomb the morning of the Resurrection, and she helped carry the word to the disciples (Luke 24:10).

NICODEMUS *(meaning* **conqueror of the people***) A Pharisee, a member of the Sanhedrin, a leader of the people.*

Nicodemus showed interest in Jesus. He came to ask Jesus questions, though he came in the middle of the night, probably knowing it wasn't safe to be seen with Jesus (John 3:1-21).

Nicodemus might have been a man who believed but did not actually join the disciples. He defended Jesus before the Sanhedrin, stating that their law didn't judge people without a hearing (John 7:45-52).

Nicodemus provided a hundred pounds of myrrh and aloes for Jesus' burial, thus indicating that he was a rich man (John 19:38-39).

Fruit of the Spirit Cards

LOVE

JOY

PEACE

PATIENCE

KINDNESS

GENEROSITY

FAITHFULNESS

GENTLENESS

SELF-CONTROL

Bible People of Faith

JOSEPH OF ARIMATHEA
A secret disciple of Jesus. Joseph of Arimathea is thought to have been rich. He had a rock-hewn gravesite in a good location, and that itself was an indication of wealth.

Joseph was probably a member of the Sanhedrin. We know he was a secret disciple of Jesus. He had purchased a new burial place when he moved to Jerusalem from Arimathea.

Jewish law required that criminals be buried on the day of their death. Joseph volunteered his unused burial site. Nicodemus helped Joseph of Arimathea take Jesus' body and wrap it for burial (John 19:38-42).

All four Gospels list Joseph as the man who offered his grave for Jesus' burial.

SIMON OF CYRENE
A man from Cyrene in North Africa.

Simon was most likely a disciple. His sons, Alexander and Rufus, are mentioned by Mark, and that probably means that they were known to the early Christian church.

Since the main post of the cross would have already been in the ground, this meant that Jesus was carrying (and Simon took over carrying) the crossbar for the cross.

This story is told in Matthew 27:32; Mark 15:21, and Luke 23:26. John says that Jesus carried the cross himself.

CENTURION AT THE CROSS
A commander of a Roman **centuria***. Though it means one hundred, a* **centuria** *was usually about eighty soldiers.*

Centurions held a high status in society.

The New Testament often speaks well of centurions. Cornelius (page 135) was a centurion, as was the centurion who believed in Jesus enough to ask him to heal his servant by speaking, knowing that Jesus did not have to be present to heal.

At the foot of the cross an unnamed centurion and those who were with him (probably his soldiers) witnessed Jesus' death and experienced the earthquake. The centurion's reaction was to say, "Truly this man was God's Son!" (Matthew 27:54). Was this a conversion at the foot of the cross?

Activity: Repent and Repay

As sinners we repent and God forgives us. But our repentance must be sincere, and there are still consequences for our actions that we cannot change. However, when we truly repent, we try to turn our lives around. What is the first step we can take to turn our lives around?

Zacchaeus is a good example. As a chief tax collector he had made himself rich by regularly overcharging on taxes. It was a common practice and expected by everyone, especially his victims. After repenting, what did Zacchaeus do? He gave half of his possessions to the poor, and to those he had cheated he paid back four times as much.

Peter denied Jesus three times. Peter repented of his sin against the Son of God. What did he do as repayment? He never denied Jesus again, and he carried the story of the good news to all who would listen.

• Divide participants into small groups.

• Read from the following actions.

• Have groups decide on one way the person can begin to turn his or her life around by repaying for past actions.

• When groups have decided, let them share their decisions, then give them another action.

1. You kept the money when the cashier made a mistake and gave you too much change.

2. You lied to your teacher (or boss) about not being at school (work), saying you were sick when you really just didn't want to go.

3. You gossiped about Mrs. Jones, repeating what you heard someone else say about her. Later you found out what you said was not true.

4. You were really angry with Tom Smith, who always pushes people around, so you let the air out of his tires.

5. You photocopied music for your church to use in worship even though your church has not purchased a license to photocopy music.

7. You made fun of someone in your Sunday school class because he (she) said something that you thought sounded really stupid. Others must have thought so too because they laughed with you.

8. You promised your friend you would help him (her) with something. And then you got an opportunity to do something that sounded like more fun. You didn't want to hurt your friend's feelings, so you lied about about why you were breaking your promise.

Bible People of Faith

The
Early
Church

Activity: Form a Faith Community

Early Christians had to develop their own form of worship and their own way of meeting the needs of the faithful as well as relating to the world. Challenge participants to think through all the faith issues of life by working together to form their own faith community. This day retreat is meant for 10-year-olds and up. Be sure there are sufficient breaks and meals.

• Read aloud Acts 2:43-47.

• Tell participants that they are starting from scratch. They are to form a community in which they can worship, encourage each other in their daily lives, and carry the good news to others. Ask for ideas on how to begin.

• If they have ideas, let them run with one they choose (unless it's just replicating their own church).

If they don't know where to begin, use the following process:

• Work together to write a statement of belief. Begin with brainstorming and writing ideas on newsprint.

• Looking at the statement, come up with a list on another sheet of newsprint of what types of activities or events must take place to maintain a faithful life according to the statement of belief.

• Divide up into small groups. Hand out a copy of the reproducible on page 122 to each group.

• Ask the group to answer the questions on the page and then to use a sheet of newsprint and a marker to sketch out their organizational plan.

• Bring the groups back together, post the plans, and have a spokesperson from each group share their plan.

• Look at the common parts of the plans and list those on a separate sheet of paper.

• Lead a discussion on the parts of the plans that do not agree. Is there room for compromise? Work together to come to a consensus about the differing issues.

• Ask a volunteer to read aloud Acts 6:1-7. Then ask participants to decide on a method(s) to carry out the tasks at hand. You need people to fill certain functions. How will you find those people?

• Depending upon decisions made, choose participants to plan and present a closing worship.

STEPHEN *(meaning **crown**). The first Christian martyr and a very important person in the change of Christianity from a small sect of Judaism in Jerusalem into a growing religion carried to other parts of the world.*

Stephen's story is told only in the Book of Acts.

Stephen was a Hellenist, a Greek-speaking Jew.

Stephen's story begins in Acts 6:1-7. In the early days of the church, conflict arose. The number of converts was growing and the Hellenists complained against the Hebrews because the Hellenist widows weren't getting their share of the daily food.

The twelve disciples called the whole community together and told them to select seven good men, full of the Spirit and of wisdom. These seven were set aside to devote themselves to prayer and to serve the community. The community chose Stephen, a man full of faith and the Holy Spirit, and six other men to serve the church.

Stephen was an important figure to the first-century Christians. Acts 6:8 says Stephen was "full of grace and power." It also says he did many signs and wonders among the people.

However, Stephen was not popular with everybody. He predicted that the Temple would be destroyed. He was brought before the council on a charge of blasphemy (speaking against God). Stephen defended himself by recounting the history of the Hebrew people and their continual disobedience to God. It took him a long time—53 verses of Acts 7. And perhaps the best defense is not to attack those bringing charges against you.

Stephen was convicted and condemned to death by stoning. As the stoning began, Stephen was filled with the Holy Spirit and saw Jesus standing at the right hand of God. As they continued to stone him, he repeated Jesus' prayer from the cross, "Do not hold this sin against them."

Saul was standing and watching the stoning, and he approved. With Stephen's death persecution of the Christian church in Jerusalem began. It became so bad that Christians scattered, but they carried their belief in the risen Christ with them, and Christianity began to spread (Acts 8:1-4).

Activity: Form a Faith Community Questions

Answering the following questions will help you make decisions about your faith community.

1. What basic beliefs does your group hold?

2. How do you want to honor/worship God?

3. Look at your beliefs. What other things does your Christian community need to do to live out its beliefs?

4. How will your Christian community deal with problems?

5. How will your Christian community reach out to others? (Or will it want to keep others out of the community?)

6. When you come together, where will you meet?

7. What kinds of things will need to be done for your Christian community to survive?

8. What kind of responsibilities does your Christian community have to people outside the community?

PAUL

PAUL **Paul** *was his Greek name,* **Saul** *his Hebrew name. Paul was the man who had the greatest influence in changing Christianity from a small Jewish sect into a separate world religion.*

Born in Tarsus, a Roman citizen with a good education, Paul was a Jew, a Pharisee, and a persecutor of Christians. He was at the stoning of Stephen and approved of it. He was converted to Christianity when Christ appeared to him in a blinding light on the road to Damascus.

What we know about Paul comes from the Book of Acts and Paul's thirteen letters. Paul was viewed with suspicion in Jerusalem (because of his persecution of Christians). He was the champion of the Gentiles, and the church was spread by Paul through three missionary journeys (see map on page 125). When Paul and Barnabas (first missionary journey) arrived in a new location, they would preach first at the Jewish synagogue until the Jewish crowds would get angry and throw them out. They then would take their message to the Gentiles.

Paul was finally arrested and he appealed to the emperor. He was imprisoned. The New Testament does not actually tell us what happened to Paul, but tradition tells us that he was executed sometime after A.D. 60. Paul's story is a long and complicated one. You can learn more about him by reading about the people associated with him.

Some Main Events of Paul's Story

- Saul watches the stoning of Stephen and approves of it (Acts 8:1).

- Saul persecutes Christians and helps drag them off to prison (Acts 8:2-3).

- Saul asks for letters to the synagogues in Damascus so that he might arrest more Christians. On his way to Damascus Jesus appears to him in a blinding light. He is temporarily blinded (Acts 9:1-9).

- Ananias reluctantly restores Saul's sight. Saul is baptized (Acts 9:10-19). Saul preaches in Damascus and has to escape being killed (Acts 9:20-25).

- Saul attempts to join the disciples in Jerusalem, but is distrusted by them and sent to Tarsus (Acts 9:26-30).

- Paul and Barnabas are sent from Antioch with an offering for the church in Judea (Acts 11:27-30).

- Paul and Barnabas are commissioned by the church in Antioch and go on a missionary journey (Acts 13–14). (See the map on page 125.)

- John Mark, a helper, leaves Paul and Barnabas at Perga and returns to Jerusalem (Acts 13:13).

- The council in Jerusalem debates the necessity of Gentiles first being circumcised to become Christians. Paul argues that salvation comes through grace. Paul, Barnabas, and Silas are commissioned to carry letters to the church (Acts 15:1-35).

- Paul and Barnabas argue over John Mark and decide to separate (Acts 15:36-41).

- Paul goes on his second missionary journey accompanied by Silas, and later Timothy (Acts 15:40–18:22). (See the map on page 125.)

- Paul's third missionary journey may have taken place because of a problem in the church at Ephesus (Acts 18:24–19:41).

- Paul journeys back to Jerusalem (Acts 21:1-16).

- Paul is arrested in the Temple. He is taken before Felix, the governor, and is imprisoned at Caesarea (Acts 21:27–26:32).

- Paul sails for Rome and is shipwrecked on Malta (Acts 27:1–28:10).

- Paul is imprisoned in Rome and continues to preach (Acts 28:11-31).

Activity: Meet Paul

Paul went on three missionary journeys. Along the way, he met some pretty interesting people. Match the Bible references with the person and the place. Names may be used more than once. *(Answers are on page 155.)*

Saul and _____ were set apart for God's work at the church in

_____. (Acts 13:1-2)

When Paul and Barnabas arrived in _____, they proclaimed the

word of God. They had _____ to assist them. (Acts 13:5)

Judas (Barsabbas) and _____ were chosen along with Paul

and Barnabas to carry a letter from the council of _____ to

_____. (Acts 15:22)

_____ was a young convert from _____

who became Paul's traveling companion. (Acts 16:1-2)

A seller of purple cloth, _____ was a woman from

_____. She and her whole household were converted by

Paul in _____. (Acts 16:11-15)

Paul left _____ and sailed for _____ accompanied

by _____ and _____. (Acts 18:18)

_____ and _____ were two women who lived in

Lystra. (2 Timothy 1:5)

Antioch
Corinth
Jerusalem
Lystra
Philippi
Salamis
Syria
Thyatira

Aquila
Barnabas
Eunice
John (full name: John Mark)
Lois
Lydia
Priscilla
Silas
Timothy

Bible People of Faith

PAUL'S JOURNEYS

1st Journey in **RED**

2nd Journey in **GREEN**

3rd Journey in **PURPLE**

SCALE OF MILES

0 50 100 200 300 400

Activity: How to Make a Jesse Tree

Jesse was the father of King David. The Jesse tree is a tree of symbols that help us focus on the true meaning of Advent, the coming of the promised Messiah. It is not a true "family" tree in that people are not in the direct line of descent, but it is a tree of those who are connected to Jesus, the Messiah.

Make a Jesse tree to help visualize the connection between Jesus and others who came before.

Choose one of these methods for making your tree.

Option 1: Use an artificial Christmas tree, a dead bush in a bucket or pot of soil, or a couple of large branches standing in sand (you might wish to tie them to the sides of a bucket or container for security).

Option 2: Provide a large sheet of butcher block paper and draw by hand a tree trunk and limbs (adding leaves if desired). Participants can color in the tree and tree limbs with markers. The tree will need several limbs so that you can glue symbols to them.

Option 3: Use old paper grocery bags twisted together to form a tree trunk and branches that you can attach to the wall.

See instructions for making ornaments on page 128.

ANANIAS *(meaning **Yahweh has been gracious**) A disciple in*
Damascus. The Lord came to him in a vision telling him to get up and go to a street called Straight, to the house of Judas, and to look for a man of Tarsus named Saul. Ananias protested because of the evil things Saul had done in persecuting Christians. But the Lord again said to go, for the Lord had chosen Saul to be an instrument for the spreading of the faith.

Ananias did as he was told. He went to Paul and baptized him (Acts 9:10-19a).

Do not confuse this Ananias with two scoundrels by this name in the Book of Acts.

SILAS *(Also known as **Silvanus**) A man of the Jerusalem church. At the Jerusalem Conference, Silas was chosen along with Barnabas and Paul to carry the agreement to Antioch.*

When Barnabas and Paul split up, Silas continued to travel with Paul. Like Paul he was a Roman citizen.

In Philippi Silas was thrown into prison along with Paul when Paul healed a slave girl of a demon, and her master could no longer make money from her fortunetelling.

We know Silas was still with Paul when First and Second Thessalonians were written, as these Letters came from Paul, Silvanus, and Timothy (1 Thessalonians and 2 Thessalonians 1:1—salutation). What happened to Silas after Corinth we're not sure, but he either acted as Peter's scribe or courier for First Peter (1 Peter 5:12).

JOHN MARK *An early Jewish Christian. He was probably from a family that was well off. His mother was Mary, in whose house Christians gathered to pray for Peter when he was in prison (Acts 12:12). John Mark was a cousin of Barnabas.*

John Mark traveled with Paul and Barnabas. For unknown reasons he left them at Perga and returned to Jerusalem (Acts 13:13). Paul considered this desertion and refused to travel with him again. This caused a rift between Paul and Barnabas. However, Paul seems to have later forgiven John Mark, for he is mentioned positively in Colossians 4:10 and Philemon 24.

Tradition says that John Mark is the author of the Gospel According to Mark.

Activity: Make Jesse Tree Ornaments

On a Jesse tree each person is represented by a different symbol. The symbol patterns are on pages 130, 132, 134, 136, 138, and 140. Choose one of these methods (or one of your own) for making Jesse tree ornaments. The ornaments should be very colorful.

Option 1: Place pattern on a colored felt square. Cut around pattern. Using a paper punch, punch a hole in the top and thread yarn through it to hang the ornament.

Option 2: Place pattern on two colored felt squares. Cut around pattern. Use a needle and thread to stitch three sides of the felt ornament together, leaving a hole at the top. Stuff with batting. Cut a piece of yarn for the hanger. Double yarn over, placing the two ends into the edge of the opening in the ornament. Sew the ornament shut. Hang from loop.

Option 3: Use cardstock. Cut out ornament. Decorate with paint and glitter. Using hole punch, punch a hole in the top and thread yarn through it.

Option 4: Cut ornaments out of Christmas wrapping paper. Using a hole punch, punch a hole in the top and thread ribbon through it for hanging the ornament.

Option 5: Place pattern on styrofoam and cut out with a box cutter. (This part should be done by adults.) Decorate with glue, bits of cloth or trim, and sequins. Use an ice pick or sharp knife (again, an adult must do this portion) and make a hole in the top. Use ribbon to thread through the hole for the hanging loop.

Option 6: For young children cut ornaments out of white paper and let them color the ornaments.

apple	Adam and Eve
ark	Noah
tent	Abraham & Sarah
ladder	Jacob
biblical lamp	Samuel
raven	Elijah
ram	Isaac
stone tablets	Moses
long-sleeved coat	Joseph
hand and dove	Elisha
crown	Solomon
open Bible (God's Word)	Jeremiah
harp	David
angel	the angel Gabriel
lily	Mary
rose	Isaiah
star	wise men
altar	Zechariah & Elizabeth
scalloped shell	John the Baptist
Chi Rho	Jesus
12-pointed star	the disciples
shepherd's staff	the shepherds

Bible People of Faith

BARNABAS *Joseph Barnabas (meaning* **son of encouragement** *according to Acts 4:36). An important very early convert to Christianity. He was from Cyprus (Acts 4:36).*

We know that he must have been a man with some wealth because he sold a field and gave the money for the support of the early church (Acts 4:37).

Barnabas spoke in Paul's favor when Paul first went to Jerusalem to meet with the apostles. They were suspicious of Paul because his past record of persecuting Christians was well known to them. Barnabas vouched for Paul's sincerity (Acts 9:27).

Barnabas was a leader in the early church and traveled with Paul on his first missionary journey. Barnabas had a prominent position as shown in Acts 14:8-20. Paul and Barnabas were mistaken for gods while in Iconium. Paul was mistaken for Hermes, the messenger, and Barnabas was mistaken for Zeus, the chief Greek god.

Paul and Barnabas parted ways in a dispute over John Mark. Barnabas and John Mark sailed for Cyprus (Acts 15:36-41). We do not know what happened to Barnabas after this.

Some Main Events of Barnabas' Story

- Barnabas sells his field and gives the money to the apostles (Acts 4:37).

- Barnabas speaks to the disciples in Paul's favor (Acts 9:27).

- Barnabas is sent to Antioch where he becomes a leader in the church. He brings Paul to Antioch (Acts 11:19-30).

- Barnabas and Paul are set apart by the Holy Spirit (Acts 13:1-3).

- Paul and Barnabas preach in Antioch, first to the Jews and then to the Gentiles (Acts 13:13-52).

- Paul and Barnabas are commissioned by the church in Antioch and go on a missionary journey (Acts 13–14).

- John Mark, a helper, leaves Paul and Barnabas at Perga and returns to Jerusalem (Acts 13:13).

- The council in Jerusalem debates the necessity of Gentiles first being circumcised to become Christians. Paul argues that salvation comes through grace. Paul, Barnabas, and Silas are commissioned to carry letters to the church (Acts 15:1-35).

- Paul and Barnabas argue over John Mark and decide to separate (Acts 15:36-41).

- Barnabas and John Mark sail for Cyprus (Acts 15:36-41).

Bible People of Faith

TIMOTHY *A young Gentile convert from Lystra. The son of a Jewish Christian mother and a Greek father (Acts 16:1). Timothy had a good reputation among the believers in Lystra and Iconium.*

Paul asked Timothy to accompany him on his second missionary journey, but first had him circumcised (Acts 16:3), maybe to help quiet criticism from Jewish Christians because Timothy's father was a Greek.

Timothy was sent to settle a dispute in Thessalonica and was successful (1 Thessalonians 3). He was then sent to Corinth and was not successful there (1 Corinthians 4:17-18). However, Paul and the early church still thought well of him.

Timothy was with Paul when he wrote Letters such as Romans (16:21), 1 Corinthians 1:1), and Philippians (1:1).

Paul encouraged Timothy in two Letters of the New Testament.

Timothy was imprisoned at one time and set free (Hebrews 13:23). We do not know what happened to Timothy after this.

Some Main Events of Timothy's Story

- Timothy is raised by his Jewish Christian mother and his grandmother, and grows into a respected church leader in Lystra and Iconium (2 Timothy 1:5; Acts 16:1-2).

- Paul decides to take Timothy with him on his second missionary journey, but first has Timothy circumcised (Acts 16:3).

- Timothy is sent to Thessalonica to help solve a problem there. He succeeds there (1 Thessalonians 1:1, 3).

- Timothy is set apart for his missionary work (1 Timothy 1:18; 4:14).

- Timothy is sent to Corinth to help solve a problem there. This time he does not succeed (1 Corinthians 4:17-18).

- Timothy is with Paul when he sets out for Jerusalem to take the offering from Antioch (Romans 16:21).

- Timothy is with Paul when several of his Letters are written (see above).

- Paul leaves Timothy at Ephesus to encourage and instruct the people in the church there (1 Timothy 1:3). Paul feels that Timothy needs encouragement.

- Timothy is imprisoned and released (Hebrews 13:23).

Bible People of Faith

EUNICE *Mother of Timothy. A Jewish woman who lived in Lystra. She was married to a Greek.*

Eunice was probably converted by Paul during his first missionary journey (Acts:14:6, 21-22).

Some scholars suspect that Eunice was not careful to follow all Jewish law because she married a Gentile and did not have her son Timothy circumcised (Acts 16:1-3).

Eunice is most noted for raising her son in the Christian faith (2 Timothy 1:5).

LOIS *Timothy's grandmother. She lived in Lystra and was a Christian convert. She is mentioned in the Bible only in 2 Timothy 1:5, where it says that the faith first lived in Timothy's grandmother Lois, then in his mother, Eunice, and now in Timothy.*

DORCAS *(meaning **gazelle**). Also known as **Tabitha** (in Aramaic). A Christian disciple in the city of Joppa. Her story is told in Acts 9:36-43.*

Dorcas was well known for her good works and acts of charity, especially making tunics and other clothing for the poor.

Dorcas fell ill and died. The disciples sent two men for Peter, who raised her from the dead. This healing story became well known, and because of it many people were converted to the Christian faith.

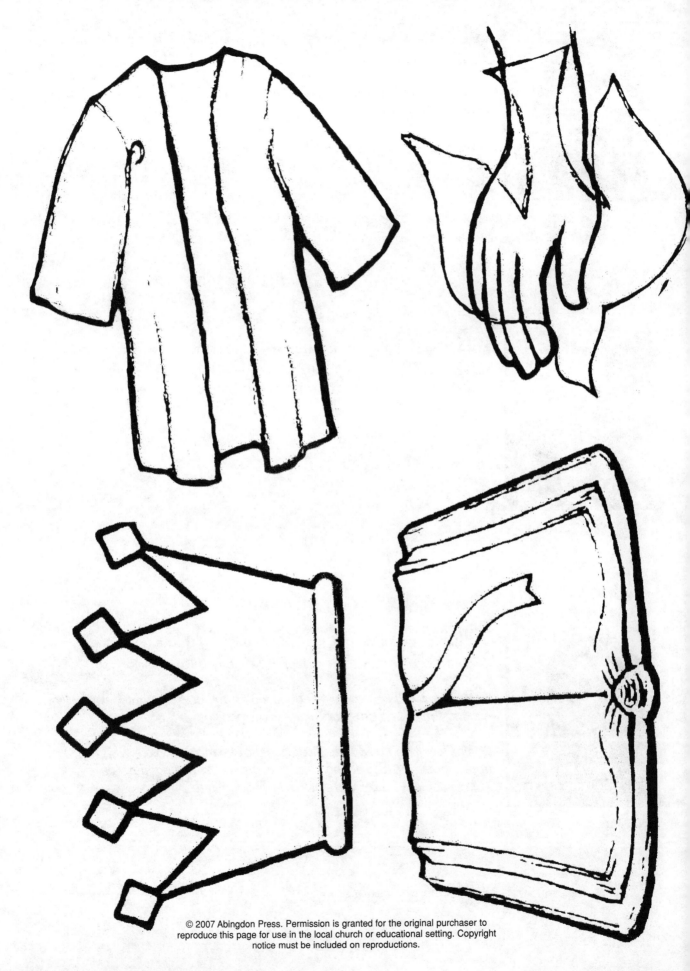

Bible People of Faith

THE ETHIOPIAN EUNUCH

A high court official in the court of the Ethiopian queen, Candace. He was in charge of the entire treasury.

The Ethiopian eunuch had come to Jerusalem to worship. As a eunuch, he would have been kept from participating in Jewish rituals.

He was studying the Scriptures and asked Philip for help in understanding what he was reading. The Ethiopian eunuch was baptized by Philip, after which Philip was snatched away. Even though the eunuch could not see Philip anymore, he went away rejoicing.

His story is told in Acts 8:26-40.

CORNELIUS

A Roman centurion in Caesarea. A **God-fearer** *(a Gentile who observed many of the Jewish religious practices). His story is told in Acts 10. He is often considered the first Gentile to convert to Christianity.*

One afternoon at about three o'clock, Cornelius had a vision in which he saw an angel of the Lord. He was told to go to Simon Peter.

At the same time Peter had a vision. Then Peter was invited by Cornelius to come to his house. At Cornelius' house Peter preached a great sermon to Cornelius, his servants, and his close friends. The Holy Spirit poured out on them, and they spoke in tongues extolling God. They were baptized into the faith.

RHODA

(meaning **rose***). A maid in the house of Mary, mother of John Mark. Her story is in Acts 12:6-18. The story is really Peter's story.*

When Peter was arrested, many early Christians gathered at Mary's home to pray for Peter. When Peter was freed by an angel of the Lord, he made his way to Mary's house. Peter knocked on the outer gate. Rhoda came to answer the knock and recognized Peter's voice. Instead of opening the gate, Rhoda ran into the house to announce Peter was free, leaving poor Peter standing on the other side of the gate still trying to get in.

Rhoda is not mentioned anywhere else in the Bible, but this is a delightful story and tells us something of the social standing of John Mark.

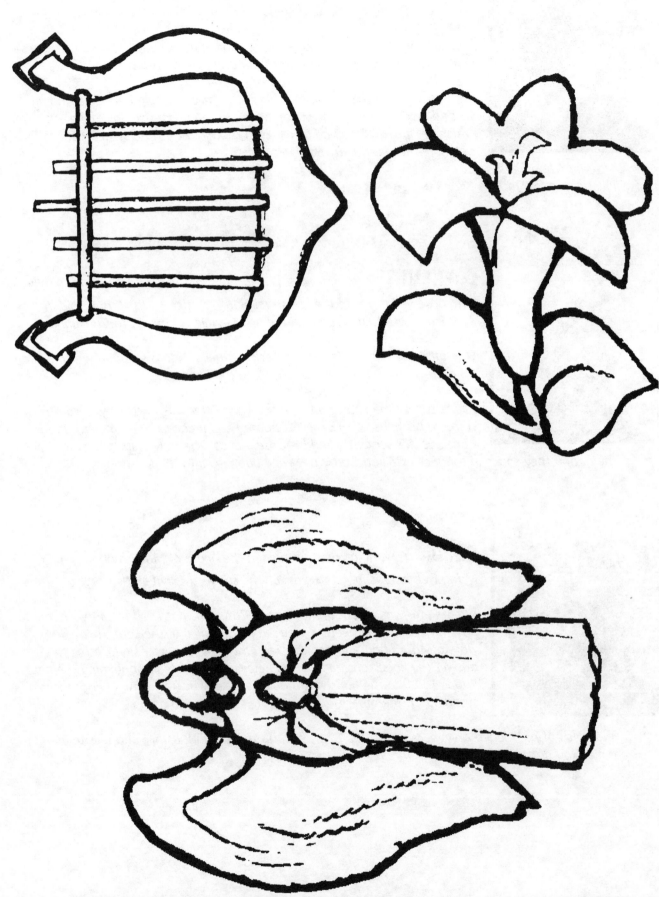

Bible People of Faith

LYDIA

A woman from Thyatira who was a seller of purple cloth. Since purple cloth was very expensive, Lydia was probably rich. And because she was the head of a household, she was probably single or perhaps a widow.

She was also a "worshiper of God," a Gentile who worshiped with Jews but probably had not converted to Judaism. She was living in Philippi when she was converted by Paul. Her entire household was baptized with her. She then opened her home to Paul and those traveling with him as an act of hospitality (Acts 16:11-15).

After Paul and Silas were released from prison, they briefly used Lydia's home as a headquarters in Philippi (Acts 16:40).

PRISCA AND AQUILA

(Prisca is the formal form of the name and Priscilla the familiar form) A wife and husband team. They were converted to Christianity before they met Paul in Corinth on his second missionary journey.

Aquila was a tent maker (or perhaps leather worker). They went to Corinth from Rome when all Christians were ordered to leave Rome (Acts 18:1-3). Prisca and Aquila were travelers. We know that at some point they were back in Rome.

They had influence in the church, as they helped guide Apollos to a better understanding of the faith (Acts 18:18-28). They put themselves in danger to help Paul (Romans 16:3-4). They had a church in their home (1 Corinthians 16:19).

EUTYCHUS

*(a common Greek name meaning **lucky** or **fortunate**)*

Eutychus was indeed lucky! When preparing to leave Troas, Paul attended a meeting at which he spoke for a long, long time. Eutychus was sitting in a window seat. Paul's speech went on so long that Eutychus got drowsy and fell out of the window which was three floors above the ground (Acts 20:7-12).

Eutychus was picked up dead. But Paul took him in his arms and said, "Do not be alarmed, for his life is in him." It is unclear whether the miracle was that Paul raised him from the dead or that Eutychus actually survived the fall.

Either way, Paul went back to the meeting, was fed, and stayed to talk. (The true moral of this story might be, don't sit in a window during a long-winded speech!)

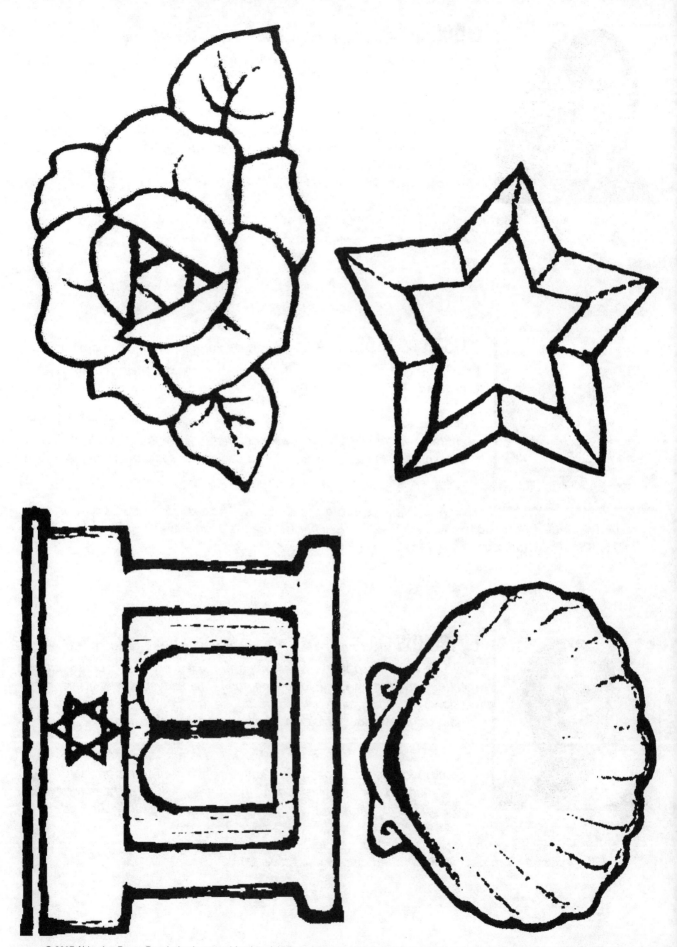

Bible People of Faith

CHLOE *A woman from Corinth who got a message to Paul about the quarrels in the Corinthian church. She might have had a large family or been the head of a household of slaves or servants (1 Corinthians 1:11), for it was "Chloe's people" who got the report to Paul.*

There have been many guesses about Chloe, but we really do not know anything else about her.

PHILEMON *Owner of the slave Onesimus. A Christian. He received a letter from Paul.*

Apphia and Archippus might be Philemon's wife and son (Philemon 2). Since Archippus lived with Philemon and Archippus lived in Colossae (Colossians 4:17), then it seems Philemon probably lived in Colossae.

Philemon was asked by Paul to allow his slave Onesimus to be set free and even to return to Paul in Rome.

ONESIMUS *(meaning **useful**) A slave belonging to Philemon. He ran away to Rome. (It is thought perhaps he had stolen from Philemon before he ran.)*

In Rome Onesimus met Paul and was converted. Paul sent Onesimus back to Philemon with a letter asking that Philemon set Onesimus free and send him back to Paul.

*Paul plays on the meaning of Onesimus' name (**useful**) in his Letter to Philemon (Philemon 11).*

Bible People of Faith

Bible People of Faith

JAMES

BARTHOLOMEW

ANDREW

JUDAS SON
OF JAMES

JOHN

JAMES SON
OF ALPHAEUS

PHILIP

PETER

MATTHEW

JUDAS
ISCARIOT

THOMAS

SIMON
THE ZEALOT

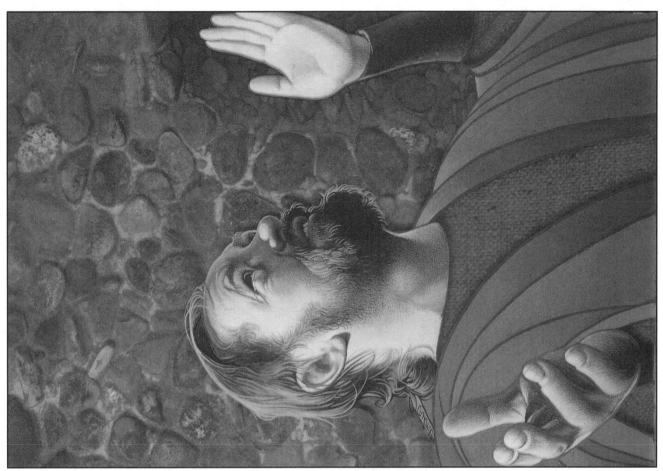

Bible People of Faith

PETER

PAUL

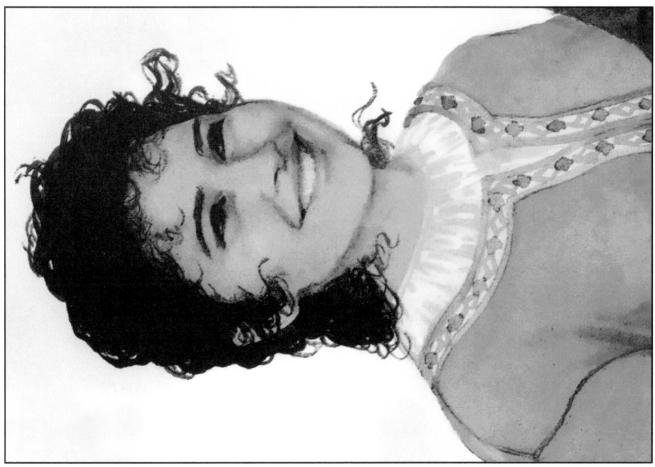

JOHN THE BAPTIST

MARY

Bible People of Faith

MARY OF BETHANY

MARY MAGDALENE

LAZARUS

MARTHA

Bible People of Faith

CORNELIUS   NICODEMUS

CENTURION AT THE CROSS

Bible People of Faith

BARNABAS

STEPHEN

LYDIA

TIMOTHY

Bible People of Faith

RHODA

DORCAS

JOHN MARK

THE ETHIOPIAN EUNUCH

Answers to "Meet Paul," p. 124

Saul and **BARNABAS** were set apart for God's work at the church in **ANTIOCH**. (Acts 13:1-2)

When Paul and Barnabas arrived in **SALAMIS**, they proclaimed the word of God. They had **JOHN** to assist them. (Acts 13:5)

Judas (Barsabbas) and **SILAS** were chosen along with Paul and Barnabas to carry a letter from the council of **JERUSALEM** to **ANTIOCH**. (Acts 15:22)

TIMOTHY was a young convert from **LYSTRA** who became Paul's traveling companion. (Acts 16:1-2)

A seller of purple cloth, **LYDIA** was a woman from **THYATIRA**. She and her whole household were converted by Paul in **PHILIPPI**. (Acts 16:11-15)

Paul left **CORINTH** and sailed for **SYRIA**, accompanied by **PRISCILLA** and **AQUILA**. (Acts 18:18)

LOIS and **EUNICE** were two women who lived in Lystra. (2 Timothy 1:5)

Pictorial Timeline

If you would like to use some people from your "Bible People Art Gallery" as part of a timeline, here are some dates:

• Prehistory	Creation
	Noah and the Flood
• about 2100 B.C.	Abraham travels to Canaan
• before 1650 B.C.	Joseph's family moves to Egypt
• about 1650-1250 B.C.	the Hebrews become slaves in Egypt
• about 1350 B.C.	Moses is born
• about 1250 B.C.	The Exodus from Egypt
• about 1200 B.C.	Israelites enter the Promised Land
• about 1200-1000 B.C.	Judges lead Israel
• about 1000 B.C.	United Kingdom
• about 900 B.C	Divided Kingdom
• 700 B.C.	End of Northern Kingdom; the Exile
• about 530 B.C.	Return from Exile
• about 6 B.C.	Jesus' birth
• A.D. about 30-33	Crucifixion and Resurrection of Jesus
• A.D. about 40-50	Paul's Letters
• A.D. about 60-90	The Gospels

BIBLIOGRAPHY

Bible Teacher Kit (Abingdon Press, 1994).

Chronological and Background Charts of the New Testament, by H. Wayne House (The Zondervan Corporation, 1981).

Dictionary of Bible and Religion, The, William H. Gentz, general editor (Abingdon Press, 1986).

Eerdmans Bible Dictionary, The, Allen C. Myers, revision editor (William B. Eerdmans Publishing Company, 1987).

Eerdmans Dictionary of the Bible, David Noel Freedman, editor (William B. Eerdmans Publishing Company, 2000).

Gospel Parallels: A Synopsis of the First Three Gospels, Burton H. Throckmorton, Jr., editor (Thomas Nelson Publishers, 1979).

Holman Book of Biblical Charts, Maps, and Reconstructions, Marsha A. Ellis Smith, general editor (Broadman & Holman Publishers, 1993).

Illustrated Bible Dictionary, The: Parts I, 2, and 3, coordination by Derek Wood (Inter-Varsity Press, 1980).

Jesse Tree, The: The Heritage of Jesus in Stories and Symbols of Advent for the Family, by Raymond and Georgene Anderson (Fortress Press, 1966).

New Interpreter's Bible, The: A Commentary in Twelve Volumes, Editorial Board: Leander E. Keck, convener and senior New Testament editor (Abingdon Press, 1994-1998).

New Revised Standard Version Concordance Unabridged, The, by John R. Kohlenberge III (The Zondervan Corporation, 1991).

Oxford Companion to the Bible, The, Bruce M. Metzger and Michael D. Coogan, editors, (Oxford University Press, 1993).

People From the Bible, by Martin Woodrow (Old Testament) and E.P. Sanders (New Testament) (Eurobook Limited, 1987).

Seasons of Faith: Teaching the Christian Year, by Marcia Stoner (Abingdon Press, 2003).

Symbols of Faith: Teaching Images of the Christian Faith, by Marcia Stoner (Abingdon Press, 2001).

Tyndale Handbook of Bible Charts & Maps, Neil S. Wilson and Linda K. Taylor (Tyndale House Publishers, 2001).

United Methodist Book of Worship, The (The United Methodist Publishing House, 1992).

World's Bible Handbook, by Robert T. Boyd (World Bible Publishers, Inc., 1991).

CREDITS

Text credit: p. 126: Modified from "Make Jesse Tree Ornaments," EXPLORING FAITH: TWEENS IN TRANSITION®, Teacher, Fall 2006, p. 78, © 2006 Cokesbury

Art and photo credits:

pp. 7, 25 (Sarah and Abraham), pp. 7, 27 (Isaac, Rebekah), pp. 9, 31 (Rachel), p. 39 (Miriam), p. 50 (Mephibosheth, Absalom), p. 51 (Abigail, Bathsheba, Nathan), p. 73 (Josiah), pp. 111, 147 (Mary Magdalene), p. 115 (Joanna): Francis Phillipps/Linden Artists, © 2004 Cokesbury

pp. 9, 29 (Jacob), pp. 9, 31 (Esau), pp. 13, 41 (Deborah), p. 31 (Leah), pp. 19, 75 (Daniel), pp. 19, 81 (Jonah), pp. 19, 69 (Jeremiah), pp. 121, 151 (Stephen), p. 127 (Silas), p. 133 (Lois), pp. 135, 153 (Ethiopian eunuch, Rhoda), p. 137 (Philemon, Onesimus): Francis Phillipps/Linden Artists, © 2001 Cokesbury

pp. 9, 41 (Joshua), pp. 109, 141 (Thomas): Adam Hook/Linden Artists, © 2006 Cokesbury

pp. 11, 33 (Joseph): Ron Hester, © 2001 Cokesbury

pp. 11, 37 (Moses): Marcy Ramsey/Portfolio Solutions, © 2007 Cokesbury

pp. 13, 45 (Samuel), pp. 15, 53 (Solomon), pp. 17, 61 (Esther), p. 39 (Aaron), p. 50 (Jonathan), p. 71 (Elisha), p. 77 (Shadrach, Meshach, Abednego), pp. 107, 141 (Andrew, Bartholomew, Judas son of James, Matthew), pp. 109, 141 (Simon the Zealot, James son of Alphaeus), pp. 111, 141 (James), pp. 123, 143 (Paul), p. 127 (Ananias), p. 133 (Eunice), pp. 133, 153 (Dorcas), pp. 135, 149 (Cornelius), p. 137 (Eutychus), pp. 139, 151 (Lydia): Francis Phillipps/Linden Artists, © 2006 Cokesbury

pp. 13, 43 (Gideon): J. William Myers, Jr., © 1997 Cokesbury

pp. 13, 43 (Samson), pp. 15, 47 (Saul), p. 83 (Zechariah): Francis Phillipps/Linden Artists, © 2003 Cokesbury

pp. 15, 49 (David), p. 82 (Habakkuk), p. 83 (Zephaniah, Haggai, Malachi), pp. 105, 141 (Judas Iscariot), pp. 109, 141 (Philip), pp. 111,141 (John): Francis Phillipps/Linden Artists, © 2005 Cokesbury

pp. 17, 57 (Ruth): Cheryl Arnemann/John Walter and Associates, © 1997 Cokesbury

pp. 17, 63 (Job): Lee Freppon, © 1997 Cokesbury

pp. 17, 59 (Ezra), pp. 19, 59 (Nehemiah): Larry Salk/Rosenthal Associates, © 1998 Abingdon Press

pp. 21, 73 (Huldah), p. 79 (Joel, Obadiah): Francis Phillipps/Linden Artists, © 2005 Cokesbury

pp. 21, 71 (Elijah): Randy Wollenmann, © 2005 Cokesbury

pp. 21, 67 (Isaiah): Richard Hook/Linden Artists, © 2004 Cokesbury

p. 24 (Adam and Eve): John Lupton/Linden Artists, © 2000 Cokesbury

p. 24 (Abel and Cain): Ron Mazellan, © 1999 Cokesbury

p. 24 (Noah's Ark): Dennis Jones, © 2006 Cokesbury

p. 41 (Rahab): Christa Hook/Linden Artists, © 2006 Cokesbury

p. 57 (Naomi): William J. Myers, © 1998 Cokesbury

p. 57 (Boaz): Francis Phillipps/Linden Artists, © 2002 Cokesbury

p. 79 (Hosea): Sandy Rabinowitz/Portfolio Solutions, © 2006 Cokesbury

p. 79 (Amos), p. 82 (Micah), pp. 113, 147 (Martha, Mary of Bethany, Lazarus), pp. 115, 149 (Nicodemus), p. 117 (Joseph of Arimathea): Richard Hook/Linden Artists, © 2002 Cokesbury

p. 82 (Nahum): Adam Hook/Linden Artists, © 2004 Cokesbury

pp. 85-86 (Genealogy): design by Vicki Williams, © 2004

p. 89 (Jesus): Larry Salk/Rosenthal Associates, © 2004 Abingdon Press

pp. 97, 145 (Mary), p. 97 (Joseph with baby Jesus): Cheryl Arnemann/John Walter and Associates, © 1996 Cokesbury

p. 99 (Zechariah and Elizabeth): Angus McBride/Linden Artists, © 2001 Cokesbury

p. 99 (Simeon and Anna): Joe Boddy, © 2006

pp. 101, 145 (John the Baptist): Marcy Ramsey, © 2007 Cokesbury

pp. 103, 141, 143 (Peter): Joanne L. Scribner/Portfolio Solutions, © 1998 Cokesbury

p. 115 (Zacchaeus): Margaret Lindmark, © 2005 Cokesbury

p. 117 (Simon of Cyrene): Robert Jefferson, © 2007 Cokesbury

pp. 117, 149 (Centurion at the Cross): Ron Mazellan, © 1998 Cokesbury

p. 125 (Paul's Journeys): Randy Wollenmann, © 2006 Cokesbury

pp. 127, 153 (John Mark): David Thompson/Linden Artists, © 2002 Cokesbury

pp. 129, 151 (Barnabas): David Thompson/Linden Artists, © 2007 Cokesbury

pp. 130, 132, 134, 136, 138, 140 (Jesse Tree Ornaments): Randy Wollenmann, © 2006 Cokesbury

pp. 131, 151 (Timothy): Cheryl Arnemann/John Walter and Associates, © 2000 Cokesbury

p. 139 (Prisca and Aquila): Adam Hook/Linden Artists, © 2007 Cokesbury

p. 139 (Chloe): Christa Hook/Linden Artists, © 2007 Cokesbury

Index of Bible People

Bold type is for "Bible People Portraits" page; *italic type is for "Who Am I?" card.*

Index of Activities, Charts, and Reproducibles